NATURAL WORLDS ❖ ROBERT BATEMAN

ROBERT BATEMAN

NATURAL WORLDS

TEXT BY RICK ARCHBOLD

A WELLFLEET PRESS /
MADISON PRESS BOOK

WELLFLEET
PRESS

This edition published in 2005 by
WELLFLEET PRESS
A divison of BOOK SALES, INC.
114 Northfield Avenue
Edison, New Jersey 08837
USA

ISBN-13: 978-0-7858-1974-5
ISBN-10: 0-7858-1974-6

Printed and bound in Singapore

Produced by:
Madison Press Books
1000 Yonge Street, Suite 200
Toronto, Ontario
Canada M4W 2K2

1 / *House Finch and Roses*, 1995
2,3 / *Catching the Light – Barn Owl*, 1988
5 / *Horned Puffins*, 1991
6,7 / *Ceremonial Pose – Red-crowned Crane*, 1991
8 / *Elephant Cow and Calf*, 1971

To my wife, Birgit, whose talents and vitality have created a wonderful world for me and our family.

CONTENTS

The Western Shore

Robert Bateman 1996

For the past decade I've lived on Canada's west coast, a land very different from southern Ontario, where I grew up and spent most of my adult life. But on Salt Spring Island my wife Birgit, our children and I have put down roots quickly. Now that I've become acquainted with the subtleties of its seasons and explored its remarkable physical and biological variety, it has become a part of me.

Salt Spring, one of the Gulf Islands lying between Vancouver Island and the British Columbia mainland, is blessed with a moderate Mediterranean climate, marked by hot dry summers and mild damp winters. On Salt Spring the contrasts come less from changes in season than from the topography. Within a very short distance you can experience a great diversity of life zones, each with its own special characteristics, ranging from the sea to remnants of the dense forest of Douglas firs that once covered the interior of the island.

I love living at the ocean's edge and manage to get out in my canoe or kayak almost every day. On a late-afternoon paddle I usually sense at some point that I am being accompanied by a silent

River Otter, 1993 (previous page)
Bateman House and Otters, 1996
Bateman Studio View, 1996

13

observer. When I turn to look, I meet the large liquid eyes of a harbor seal, who will swim along for a while, then submerge silently like a submarine periscope. If I'm lucky, I might spot a sea lion cruising by the rocks at the mouth of the bay. Quite often I'll surprise a family of river otters chirping their way along one of the pretty white-shell beaches that dot the shore.

As a lifelong birder, I'm always on the lookout for interesting species or unusual congregations. But for much of the year I see only the permanent residents, including mew and glaucous-winged gulls, black oystercatchers with their startling orange-red bills, and pelagic and double-crested

cormorants. In late summer the birding begins to get more interesting as southward-traveling migrants either stop for a few days or come to spend the winter. Among my favorite arrivals are the black turnstones, the marbled murrelets, and the big flocks of ducks, including buffleheads and American wigeons. Occasionally, when deep-swimming salmon chase a great ball of herring to the surface, the fish attract a noisy gathering of gulls, mergansers,

Golden Light – Black-tailed Fawn, 1995
Black-tailed Buck by the Ocean, 1993

15

Robert Bateman 1995 ©

cormorants, bald eagles and sometimes three types of loons.

When I haul out my canoe back home, I pass through the aromatic intertidal zone, where purple starfish creep up and down the cliff with the water's ebb and flow. The space between high tide and low tide supports a lavish concentration of life. No wonder the Haida people say, "When the tide is out, the table is set."

In spring, the cliffs above high-tide level become a colorful rock garden. Because I live on a southwest-facing slope, the spring sun quickly turns the exposed rock below my house into an incubator for plant life. The hardy sedum, with its pale turquoise leaves, bright-red stalks and yellow flowers, thrives in the most parched places. Patches of blue-eyed Mary, looking like dense beds of tiny forget-me-nots, draw moisture from mats of moss at the cliff edge. And the bright-yellow monkey flower occupies seeps in the rock: places where cracks and fissures have stored up the moisture from the winter rains.

A little higher up the trees begin: the tall straight Douglas fir, the sinuous arbutus (or madrone) with its reddish-brown bark, and the garry oak. The thin soils here support little undergrowth, creating a kind of open parkland effect. Beneath the garry oaks a profusion of wildflowers, including the beautiful sapphire-blue camas, bursts forth each spring.

Like a mouse I seem to need a network of established paths that lead from my home burrow, and the trails I design please both the artist and the naturalist in me. I make sure that each path takes advantage of every view, but I also want it to explore every habitat and give me the chance of seeing or hearing different birds and wildlife. So my route never takes me straight from A to Z, but pauses frequently as it meanders through the whole alphabet.

Glaucous-winged Gulls Resting, 1995

Salt Spring Sheep, 1991

One of my favorite trails on Salt Spring leads up over the ridge behind our house to the great stump of a Douglas fir that was

NATURAL WORLDS

Robert Bateman. 1991

probably felled sometime in the 1920s. For some reason, those early loggers never finished this particular job; what's left of the rest of the tree lies nearby and has become a nurse log for the young firs that now grow out of it. Some long-forgotten fellings like this one now lie in open meadows, where erosion has left the soils too poor to support the forest giants of old.

Much of the interior of the island was cleared for farmland long ago. In a way I enjoy this domesticated landscape as much as the wilder parts: it reminds me of landscapes I saw over the many years I lived in southern Ontario. The sheep on Salt Spring are one of our main agricultural products. The one I painted *(previous page)* has bits of straw and hay hanging from its body, and its fur is matted from wandering through underbrush and lying down in puddles. To me, its raffish appearance makes it a suitably informal Salt Spring representative.

When I'm at home, I'm usually at my easel, and I often pause in my painting to look out the studio window to take in the lovely view of the forested slopes across the bay. But the foreground of this panorama often diverts my eye, especially when a bald eagle comes to perch in the dead tree I purposely planted in cement on the rocks in front of the house. Of all the island's wilder residents, the bald eagle remains in a class of its own. Although this eagle is fairly common on the West Coast, *Kestrel and Grasshopper, 1992*

19

having suffered much less from the DDT that nearly wiped out the eastern population earlier in this century, each sighting still gives me a thrill.

Near the eagle perch I have built an otter house with a freshwater pool on its doorstep. My idea was to lure the otter family into new digs—away from their residence beneath our living room, where they had torn out all the insulation. This strategy seems finally to have succeeded. And the roof of their house, which is covered with sod and blends nicely into the landscape, has become a favorite otter hangout. After returning from a fishing expedition, the otters love to freshen up in the pool and then roll around on the sod roof, slithering and twisting at every imaginable angle, probably to groom themselves. One day last winter, after one of our rare snowfalls, nine otters cavorted on the roof in two playful, writhing heaps. The snow sent them into some kind of otter ecstasy.

Living on Salt Spring allows me to view the world with a bit of critical distance. The pace of island life is slower than on the mainland, and the rhythms of the sea, the shore and the forest are always close at hand. While I'm painting, scents and sounds waft in through the open windows of my studio. Even though I'm also surrounded by modern gadgets—phone, computer and fax machine—that defy geography, this proximity to the world as it was before technology and progress became our gods is my constant reminder of something deeper—of just how great a responsibility we have to achieve a state of peaceful coexistence between the human and the wild.

Vigilance – Bald Eagle, 1993
Tidal Zone, 1995 (overleaf)

Paddling my canoe around Salt Spring Island, I often see marbled murrelets bobbing and diving for small fish. Only recently have researchers discovered that these birds actually nest on the pads of moss growing on the high branches of ancient trees in British Columbia's old-growth forests, evidence of the interdependence of species and of the importance of virgin forest in ensuring biodiversity. These tiny relatives of the auks and puffins—almost always seen in pairs—look so unlikely riding the sea swells; I always imagine they will simply get swallowed up in the vastness of the ocean.

Marbled Murrelet, 1991
Marbled Murrelets, 1992

What attracts me to cliffside seabird colonies is their noisy, pungent concentration of communal life. Waves are crashing below, the air is filled with constant cries and calls, and the rich smell is like a combination of seafood chowder and cow manure seasoned with sea salt. Nests occupy every nook and cranny of the cliff face, and yet in a sense the whole world is only a few inches deep. Move an inch or two inward and you meet solid rock. Move an inch or two outward and you are airborne.

This fact makes visiting a seabird colony and observing its residents quite exciting and somewhat risky. In order to get a glimpse of this narrow, teeming society, you have to peer over a sheer cliff edge without falling. This can become quite a comical exercise: each time you venture a look, the puffins almost seem to say, "Oops, someone's peeking." Then they peek back. And their extraordinarily vivid clownlike faces add a note of hilarity to the whole ritual.

Tufted Puffin Portrait, 1991
Tufted Puffins, 1991

Robert Bateman 1990 ©

I have long had a passionate appreciation for the artistic achievements of indigenous people, and none more so than the magnificent totem poles carved by the native inhabitants of the northwest Pacific Coast. These exquisite abstract sculptures in wood represent for me the pinnacle of indigenous art—they are as beautiful and powerful as anything created by Picasso or Matisse. Unfortunately, the few old poles that remain in their natural settings are decaying and returning to the forest.

My visit to the now-unoccupied Haida village of Ninstints on Anthony Island at the southern tip of the Queen Charlotte Islands turned out to be one of the most moving days of my life. The surrounding virgin forest, echoing with the haunting call of the hermit thrush, inspired as much awe as a Gothic cathedral. And as I walked among the weathered old poles—some fallen, some still standing where their owners had raised them during potlatch feasts long ago—it was impossible not to feel a strong spiritual presence, a sense of connection to these great works of art, to their creators and to the primordial cosmology they evoke.

On a subsequent visit to the Queen Charlottes, a Haida elder guided Birgit and me to a secluded spot on a calm bay where Bill Reid's canoe sat at a lonely anchorage. Reid, a pioneer who has done so much to revive the ancient forms of Haida art,

directed the hollowing of the fifty-foot canoe from a single ancient red cedar according to traditional designs and following the traditional method. It was the first of its kind in almost a hundred years. Powered by twenty Haida paddlers on an epic 558-mile journey from Vancouver to Skidegate, it truly earned its name, *Loo Taa*, "Wave Eater."

Seeing the canoe was for me a kind of spiritual experience. And although there was no raven present that day, in my mind's eye I saw a raven—to the Haida the wily trickster-transformer who created the world—hovering over it, perfectly centered.

Clan of the Raven, 1990
Wave Eater and Raven Study, 1996

29

Robert Bateman 1995©

A few years ago Birgit and I had the privilege of visiting the now-empty village of 'M'imkwạmlis on Village Island, which lies off the northeast coast of Vancouver Island not far from Alert Bay. Because it was a foggy summer day, we were navigating by compass and radar over the glassy water, occasionally glimpsing the gray-green shoreline, barely aware of the muffled purring of the motor of our big old wooden boat. First the houses on the village outskirts materialized from the mist, then the lonely outline of a frontal pole appeared. These were all that remained of a traditional native house, where a noble family must have lived and held its potlatch feasts.

Of all the aboriginal inhabitants of the northwest Pacific Coast, the tribes of this area clung most tenaciously to the potlatch even after it was banned in 1885 by the Canadian government. Despite repeated attempts by local Indian agents to eliminate potlatching, which was regarded as immoral and wasteful, these feasts, accompanied by lavish gift giving and ritual dancing, continued to be held quite openly into the second decade of the twentieth century. And one of the biggest potlatches to take place on the central coast was given by Daniel Cranmer in the winter of 1921-22 at 'Mi'mkwạmlis. According to Cranmer's own account, "Three to four hundred men, women and children turned up," and an enormous quantity of goods was given away, including blankets, sacks of flour, canoes, motorboats and even pool tables.

By this time, however, the Department

Potlatch Village, 1995
Haida Carving and Fox Sparrow, 1993

31

of Indian Affairs had decided to crack down hard on the potlatch, using newly granted summary powers that enabled the Indian agent to act as both judge and jury. In 1922 a total of forty-one people who had attended the event on Village Island were charged. Those who pleaded guilty received suspended sentences. Those who refused to admit they had done anything wrong—twenty-two people in all—were sentenced to short terms in Oakalla prison. But not even this killed the potlatch; it simply went underground.

As we explored the village that day, I thought of this wrong-headed attempt to suppress native culture and lamented how much has been irretrievably lost. In the mist, the deserted decaying buildings seemed to echo with voices from a time when this was a vibrant community with ancient roots. Because it was low tide, we could see the remarkable midden of mollusk shells, bleached white by sun and saltwater, that forms the beachfront— evidence of a human presence that goes back eight thousand years.

In addition to the two totem poles still standing (they have since fallen), three smaller poles lay close together in various stages of returning to nature. One of these—the least decayed—displayed a magnificent wolf carving, representing a mythical ancestor of the pole's owner. Interestingly, one West Coast native group regards the wolf as the land equivalent of the orca, claiming that the first killer whale was a supernatural white wolf who transformed himself into a sea creature.

Beach Grass and Tree Frog, 1991

Robert Bateman 1995 ©

W e heard the orcas before we saw them. On the boat's hydrophone their squeals, squeaks, whistles and sighs sounded as if they were echoing in a cavernous space. Finally the mist lifted a little and we saw a phalanx of black dorsal fins not too far off—a family pod. Then the mist swallowed them up again.

Perhaps one of the pods we glimpsed on that magical day of whale watching belonged to a whale that researchers have named Tsitika, an orca matriarch whose life history has given me a glimpse into the orca world. Tsitika and her family belong to the northern resident population of British Columbia killer whales. They have a remarkable social system that we are just beginning to understand. We know, for example, that this population is subdivided into clans, each one consisting of a number of closely related pods that communicate by means of a common set of sounds—a dialect. In this society, the children never leave home, so a typical pod is composed of a grandmother, her sons and daughters, and several of her daughters' young children.

When Tsitika's mother died in 1989, she became matriarch of her pod, a role she can expect to play for another thirty years. (She is not yet fifty years old, and the female lifespan can reach eighty, almost twice that of males.) Until recently, this role included acting as head of the host pod for the annual summer gathering of the clans in Johnstone Strait, which funnels millions of salmon each year. Tsitika and her family almost always arrived first, as if to scout out the territory in preparation for the big event. And they always seemed to know when another pod was approaching, swimming many miles to meet it and escort it in.

Recently, however, Tsitika's pod has relinquished much of its pivotal welcoming role for reasons that can only be described as personal. In 1993, Tsitika gave birth to a stillborn calf and became somewhat withdrawn. Since then her family has tended to keep its distance during big clan gatherings and has become decidedly less social.

As Tsitika's story demonstrates, we are increasingly learning to think of animals as distinct individuals. This knowledge, it seems to me, must inevitably lead us to treat our fellow species on the planet with much greater respect.

Tsitika and Her Son – Orcas, 1995

THE WESTERN SHORE

During the 1980s, it was estimated that thirty-one thousand miles of driftnets were set each night in the Pacific. These drifting "walls of death" captured untold numbers of dolphins, whales, pelagic birds (birds of the open ocean), sharks and turtles, along with the targeted species. Thanks to a recent United Nations moratorium on driftnet fishing, this highly destructive activity has been sharply curtailed in the Pacific, though it remains a common practice in the Mediterranean. But the underlying problem of wasteful overfishing remains. In every sea and ocean of the world, the commercial fisheries are either at or over their sustainable limit. And a shocking proportion of what is caught is discarded. Conservative estimates put this "bycatch" at 20 percent of the total commercial catch.

The plight of the world's fisheries is symbolic of a much wider and more vexing problem: the industrialization of what were for many thousands of years such essentially sustainable activities as farming, forestry and fishing. Instead of treating nature with respect, we now treat it as a value-neutral commodity. Massive sums are borrowed and invested in large-scale technology, which must be constantly fed raw material in the form of crops, trees or fish in order to pay the interest on the original loans. When the "resource base" inevitably collapses, so do the economies that depend on it. It's a vicious cycle that ends in the devastation of ecosystems and the impoverishment of the planet.

Fluid Power – Orca, 1991
Driftnet, 1993

The
Great
Divide

Robert Bateman 1994

I MADE MY FIRST TRIP ACROSS THE NORTH AMERICAN CONTINENT WHEN I was twenty. After the vast emptiness of the Prairies, my heart leapt at my first glimpse of the Rocky Mountains. The sheer drama of those impossible verticals, still capped with snow even though it was early summer, gave me a sense of exhilaration that comes back each time I return.

At that time the Rockies seemed remote, massive, impregnable. Now that I have visited them many times, they seem no less astonishing but infinitely more fragile. As in the High Arctic, life maintains only a precarious foothold in the higher reaches of the highest mountains. Yet in a small hollow sheltered from the wind and open to the sun, you may find a complex tapestry of interdependent plants. Lower down, an alpine or subalpine meadow in summer can seem like a verdant oasis with its carpet of lush grasses and brilliant wildflowers dotted with leisurely grazing mountain sheep. Still, it is often warmer at higher elevations than in the valley bottoms, since valleys get less sunlight and can act as cold-air sinks. On the south-facing slopes of high meadows it can even become extremely hot. But the warmth and serenity vanish almost instantly as clouds move in and the winds whip up. In a matter of minutes you may find yourself in a cold downpour or even a summer blizzard. Then, a few moments later, the sun may return.

It was in such a meadow in Alaska's Denali National Park that I spent several wonderful hours observing a group of Dall sheep, the northern species of North American mountain sheep. In most places Dall sheep are skittish, so

Wolf Pair in Winter, 1994 (previous page)
Rocky Mountains - Dall Sheep, 1994
Stone Sheep Ram, 1978

41

I crept along very carefully in order to circle around and above to a point where I could look down on them rather than view them against the summer sky. I was feeling quite pleased with just how close I'd come, when one of the group nonchalantly got up and walked over to within a few feet of me. I'd had no idea they could be so tame.

Because such a great area of our western mountains is protected, it is still possible to experience them much as they were before the first European explorers crossed them and followed the rivers they fed to the Pacific. Not so the Great Plains. The vast interior of the continent, irreparably altered by farming and grazing, has become a mere ecological shadow of what it once was. We can only imagine the Prairies in the days when millions of buffalo and pronghorns depended on complex fertile grasslands, and wolves and grizzly bears fed on these grazers. Yet here and there vestiges of this squandered natural legacy remain, and a few species that had all but vanished have returned to their former haunts.

Grizzly and Cubs, 1992

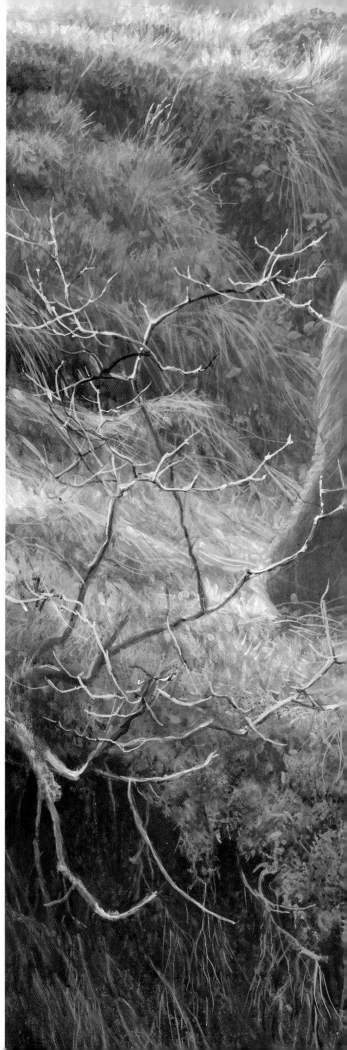

On a hike in Banff National Park quite a few years ago, my family and I found ourselves alone on a high saddle where the mountain dropped off sharply on either side. It was one of those moments when the world stands still and all your senses seem heightened. The empty space between us and the next mountain seemed almost a solid presence, so vivid was my impression of the great gulf of air.

Then I saw a hoary marmot poised atop a nearby pile of rocks. Despite its small size, it appeared to be lord and master of the high peaks that stretched off in all directions. Quietly I began moving toward it. The marmot remained motionless, allowing me to come so close I could almost touch its beautiful mantle of silvery-white fur. My attention was so focused that I was only half-conscious of a distant roaring sound—I dismissed it as a high-flying jet plane—growing gradually louder.

What happened next took only a second or two, but it seemed to stretch out over a much longer span. The marmot gave its characteristic whistle and shot down its burrow. In the split second that I cursed my bad luck, the roaring sound became so loud it seemed to come from inside my head. I looked up in time to see a golden eagle plunging across the sky so close to me that I felt the wind stirred by its dive. Then it wheeled away and soared off in search of other prey.

Hoary Marmot, 1991
Golden Eagle, 1979

44

Robert Bateman 1995 ©

Two elk feeding at the water's edge at sunset evoke a sense of almost spiritual calm. But then a faint scent or a distant sound disturbs them. They raise their heads, suddenly alert. Somewhere not far away a pack of wolves is on the trail, hunting for food. Depending on habitat, wolves prey on different grazing or browsing animals: elk, caribou, moose or deer. If there are too few wolves to keep the population in check, these herbivores can seriously damage the plant base on which they depend. And since wolves generally kill the weakest or most vulnerable members of their target group—the old and the young—they help ensure that the prey species is always at its reproductive best.

But this ecological balancing act doesn't explain why we seem to be as attracted to predators as to their victims. Wildlife artists know that images of some of the fiercest animals are among the most sought after by collectors. The wolf, with which human beings have had a long love-hate relationship, is possibly the single most popular subject of wildlife art in North America. I don't think this is because we live in an age addicted to violence: it probably has more to do with the fact that human beings once depended on hunting for survival. In some distant part of our genetic memory we can recall a time when the large predators were our rivals, and some, perhaps, even preyed on us. Could it be that we can identify with both predator and prey?

Evening Light - Elk, 1995

47

Wolf Sketch, 1990

Descending Shadows - Timber Wolves, 1995

Winter Run - Bull Moose, 1994 (overleaf)

Robert Bateman 1994 ©

Unlike most large predators, coyotes have adapted well to the human presence. Originally a western species, they have expanded their range north as far as the Arctic, south as far as the northern part of South America, and east as far as New England. When I was a boy, there were no coyotes in the ravines of Toronto. Now, I gather, they are fairly common. They are seldom seen near human habitation, however, since they are alert, nimble and usually quite shy. And though their habitat has expanded, coyotes seem most of all creatures of the open prairie, where their song—a series of sharp yelps followed by a high-pitched howl—often pierces the nocturnal stillness.

The coyote is surely one of the most adaptable predators on earth. Although its diet consists mostly of small mammals and carrion killed by larger predators, it will occasionally bring down big animals such as deer, pronghorn or young elk. And if circumstances dictate, it can survive quite nicely as a vegetarian. But part of the reason the coyote has thrived and the wolf has not may be the coyote's ability to change from life in a predominantly pack-based society to a more solitary existence. In pioneer days, coyotes were often seen in large groups. Now they generally live and hunt in nuclear family units.

The coyote is the prey of larger animals, including the wolf, the cougar, the grizzly and the black bear. So it is no wonder it does so well in neighborhoods from which these top predators have long been banished.

Gray Jay Study, 1996
Winter Trackers - Coyote, 1991

It is impossible for me to think of the buffalo, or American bison, without sadness. This charismatic creature, whose population may once have numbered as many as 60 million, was part of a temperate grasslands ecosystem unrivaled anywhere else on earth. But in an unbelievably short time—about forty years—the vast herds disappeared. At the peak of the bloody slaughter in the 1870s, perhaps as many as 2.5 million bison were killed each year, mostly for their hides, which made excellent commercial leather. This systematic annihilation opened up the prairies for settlement and at the same time solved the "Indian problem." Without the buffalo, the native way of life disappeared.

Soon after the near-elimination of the buffalo, the vast, species-rich grasslands began to fall beneath the plow. First to vanish was the tall-grass prairie, whose fertile, well-watered soils were ideal for agriculture. Less than 1 percent of North America's original tall-grass prairie survives today. The less productive grasslands, whose soil and climate made them unsuitable for cereal crops, were used for cattle—and these areas fared somewhat better. In the early days they suffered badly from overgrazing, but as succeeding generations of ranchers learned to respect nature's limits and to imitate nature's cycles, a sizable chunk of the western prairie returned to something like its original state.

The secret to saving the prairie was to make sedentary cattle behave a little like the migratory bison they replaced. The bison traveled to different pastures in different seasons, often not returning to a heavily grazed area for years, during which period it had ample time to regenerate. Modern ranchers achieve a similar effect by carefully limiting the numbers of cattle to levels that a particular piece of land can bear and by using fences and other inducements such as water and saltlicks to move the livestock around and give pastures a rest. With the help of scientists who've learned to interpret evidence of grasslands decline, the best ranchers have become increasingly sophisticated at preventing overgrazing. This system benefits both ranchers and the many bird and mammal species that have returned to the grasslands.

Wood Bison Portrait, 1984
Bison Study, 1996

Robert Bateman 1989 ©

Since 1982, more than eight hundred foxes have been released in southern Alberta and Saskatchewan, and there are now two distinct wild populations. But whether these populations will become permanent remains an open question. Recent field studies employing radio collars suggest that Canadian swift foxes may not be reproducing at the levels necessary to sustain themselves. One reason is that Prairie populations of the coyote, the swift fox's main predator, have been steadily increasing.

Unlike the swift fox, the burrowing owl never completely disappeared from Canada, but it has recently been placed on the Canadian endangered species list. This has happened despite considerable cooperation from farmers who agreed to leave parts of their land unploughed in an effort to restore the owl's habitat. More encouraging is the fact that the Canadian government has announced a ban on most uses of carbofuran, an extremely toxic pesticide that has been a major contributor to the burrowing owl's decline and to the decline of many other Prairie birds.

Curled Up - Swift Fox, 1989
Burrowing Owl Study, 1988

The plains bison is not the only species that almost disappeared after Europeans arrived on the Prairies. Just as integral a member of the mixed grasslands ecosystem was the swift fox, a nocturnal hunter no bigger than a large house cat. Despite its speed—it can run up to thirty-seven miles per hour in short bursts—and the fact that its fur was not especially prized, by 1900 only a few isolated populations remained, and by the late 1930s the swift fox had completely disappeared from the Canadian Prairies, the northern fringe of its range. In the ensuing years the U.S. population has continued to decline, but the Canadian population has recently begun to make a comeback.

A little over a decade ago, efforts were made to reintroduce the swift fox into a couple of its former Canadian haunts.

With so many species disappearing or threatened with extinction, it is always heartening to remember that some have been brought back from the brink and are now doing fairly well. One such species is the trumpeter swan, the larger of the two swans native to North America. (The other native species is the tundra swan.) The trumpeter was highly prized for its size, its meat and its down, as well as for its skin, which was used to make powder puffs. By the 1930s it had been all but wiped out east of the Rockies, but now the Pacific population is flourishing. A healthy Rocky Mountain population has been established, and efforts to reintroduce it farther east have met with some success. Even in my home province of Ontario, where circumstantial evidence suggests trumpeters once lived, the birds are making a tentative comeback. In all nearly eighteen thousand trumpeters now live in the wilds of North America, the vast majority in the Pacific Northwest, where they breed in Alaska and winter along the coasts farther south.

Trumpeter Swans in Flight, 1996
Trumpeter Swan Family, 1991

Like many North Americans of my generation I was caught up in the story of the whooping crane when I was very young. In 1941, the year it came closest to extinction, I was eleven years old and already an avid birder. Over subsequent years, as the whooping crane slowly came back, I followed its recovery and began to think that I might, after all, actually get a chance to see one of these legendary creatures, the tallest bird in North America and certainly one of the most elegant.

When the moment came, however, it took me completely by surprise. One early October in the late 1970s after Birgit and I had left teaching and were able to travel west during the fall, we took a sidetrip to Last Mountain Lake Bird Sanctuary just north of Regina, Saskatchewan. There we hoped to witness one of the great displays of North American wildlife: the annual arrival of waterfowl and sandhill cranes, which would stop to rest and feed on their way south for the winter.

As we approached the lake under a big glowering Prairie sky, I could see great flocks of flying birds: mallards, Canada geese, white-fronted geese, snow geese and sandhills. One flock was wheeling in the blustery wind while another was racing low along the horizon and yet another was coming in for a landing, only to change its collective mind at the last moment and start rising up again. The overall effect was of a constantly changing kaleidoscope of birds and scudding clouds.

Aiming for a place where sandhills were landing and taking off, we finally came upon a flock of two or three thousand birds feeding in a field not far from the lake itself. As I peered through my binoculars at this great assembly of tall gray birds, two white figures stood out like giant statues. For a moment my heart stopped. It was almost like seeing a pair of ghosts. But there was no mistaking the two tall whooping cranes with their crimson crowns and their wings tipped with black feathers. We watched them for a long time, hoping they would take flight, but they continued grazing placidly, oblivious to their fame and our continuing concern for their survival.

Crane Portrait, 1994

Marsh Edge - Whooping Cranes, 1993

I painted *Bounty of the Wetlands* to mark the removal of the white pelican from the list of Canada's endangered species in 1987. The painting's title makes the larger point that the pelican is but one of myriad plants and animals that depend on wetland environments to thrive.

Colonial water birds such as pelicans are clearly interdependent with other avian species. Part of the reason for this may simply be safety in numbers: the more birds on a nesting island the greater chance they have of fending off potential predators. And when double-crested cormorants are part of the colony, the pelicans will follow them to a food source and let the cormorants drive fish to the surface, where the pelicans can help themselves.

More than three-quarters of North American birds depend on wetlands either for breeding or as staging areas during migration. Prairie wetlands alone are the breeding grounds for more than half of all the ducks born on this continent. And most of the fish and shellfish caught in commercial fisheries depend on coastal wetlands, where they either breed or spend part of their lives. Many threatened species of plants and animals also depend on wetland areas for their survival.

Bounty of the Wetlands, 1987

The disappearance of North American wetlands is one of our most serious environmental concerns. In the United States, more than 50 percent of marshes, swamps and bogs have been drained or filled in to create farmland, new housing subdivisions, parking lots or industrial and commercial developments. In the process we are threatening biodiversity and seriously curtailing nature's ability to look after itself.

Important as the biological bounty of wetlands is, so too is their role in preventing flooding and controlling water pollution. When heavy rains fall, wetlands act like natural sponges, absorbing excess water and gradually releasing it into lakes and rivers. They also recycle nutrients, filter sediments and function as natural sewage-treatment plants. Wetlands even play a role in moderating the greenhouse effect, since they retain large quantities of carbon that would otherwise enter the atmosphere as carbon dioxide.

We have only recently come to appreciate just how important wetlands are to our environmental health. Our success in protecting them will say a lot about our commitment to handing down a livable planet to our children and grandchildren.

In His Prime - Mallard, 1993
Pintails in Spring, 1988

Robert Bateman 1988 ©

The American Southwest is a region of stark mountains, arid grasslands and vast deserts, yet it harbors an amazing variety of plants and animals. Unfortunately, among the animals we can no longer find the Mexican wolf, *el lobo*, the smallest wolf subspecies, which formerly flourished from the southwestern United States to southern Mexico. As cattle ranching expanded, the Mexican wolf declined, poisoned or shot as a threat to livestock. Although a few wild members of this vanishing race may still survive in remote parts of Mexico, there have been no recent sightings. The survival of this subspecies will therefore depend on the successful release of captive-bred wolves into safe wilderness.

In the late 1970s five wild wolves caught in Mexico became the basis of a successful captive-breeding program at the Arizona-Sonora Desert Museum near Tucson, Arizona. The danger of breeding from too small a gene pool has been alleviated by the recent discovery through genetic testing that eight wolves at the Aragon Zoo in Mexico City and fifteen more living on an Arizona ranch are also purebred members of the Mexican subspecies. If all the bureaucratic barriers can be overcome, plans call for the release of two groups of Mexican wolves in 1997 or 1998: one in southern Arizona and one in southern New Mexico. But will these captive-bred individuals readily readapt to their wild ways? No one knows for sure, though the example of the red wolf is encouraging. A small population of red wolves reintroduced in Great Smoky Mountains National Park in North Carolina quickly learned how to hunt for food and has steadily grown in number.

The decline of the Mexican wolf is a sorry chapter in a tragic tale—the virtual worldwide extermination of the wolf. In Europe only a few remnant populations remain, and in the United States this intelligent animal has been eliminated from 95 percent of its historic range.

Red Wolf, 1986
Sierra Evening - Mexican Wolf, 1993

Although my favorite environments are northern forests, misty coasts and humid rainforests, I have to confess that the desert has its appeal, especially at dawn and sunset. As in the Arctic, the wildlife is easy to see. And like plants and animals in arctic regions, the desert's inhabitants must deal with extremes of temperature and long periods without water. As long as there is some rainfall, however, deserts can support an amazing variety of life.

One of the most fascinating deserts in the world is the Sonoran Desert of the North American Southwest, which is home to a startling number of cacti, a plant family particularly well adapted to a very dry climate where rain, when it comes, usually falls in torrents. Cacti, which are succulents, can store water for long periods. They reduce transpiration to a minimum by eliminating leaves altogether and by "breathing" only at night, when they take in and store carbon dioxide for use in photosynthesis during the day.

The saguaro cactus is king of the Sonoran Desert. A saguaro can grow up to fifty feet high and live to be as many as two hundred years old. I prefer the scarred old giants to the smooth-skinned, almost modernist-looking youngsters. And the more dilapidated they become, the more likely they are to hold a nest of Gila woodpeckers, elf owls or cactus wrens.

Old Saguaro and Cactus Wrens, 1994
Gambel's Quail Portrait, 1994

The
Arctic

Robert Bateman
1996

HOW FAR NORTH MUST ONE GO TO REACH THE ARCTIC? THAT DEPENDS ON HOW YOU DEFINE IT. IN purely geographic terms, the Arctic is the area north of the Arctic Circle; in oceanographic terms, it coincides with the shifting extent of the permanent ice pack; botanically, it is the region north of the treeline. Regardless of your definition— and no one definition will do—it is a land of extremes and contradictions, of continual light and continual darkness, of frozen deserts in winter that become virtual swamps in summer, a seemingly barren place that abounds with life.

My first experience of the Arctic came in the summer of 1953 when I spent four months there as part of a geological field party mapping an iron ore formation in the Ungava Peninsula of northern Quebec. Our trip from the south had started inauspiciously and gotten worse. On the water at Lac St-Jean the pilot taxied in circles while the engine of the old Catalina flying boat coughed and sputtered, sending nauseating exhaust fumes back through the cabin. Once we finally took off, it was freezing cold in the unheated plane. Then we lurched our way through a violent thunderstorm, which sent rain through cracks in the fuselage and into the cabin, drenching us to the skin. Our party chief was sick the whole way. But when we reached our destination, our miseries were quickly forgotten.

As our aircraft descended toward the unnamed lake's surface, the long light of late afternoon illuminated a landscape of astonishing beauty. The low-angled sunlight glinted on pristine lakes and gravelly rivers, skipping across bare hills and rolling tundra that in its richness and variety reminded me of an elaborate Persian carpet made of mosses, lichens, dwarf birch and willows, and flowering plants. I felt as if I had entered not some distant region of my own country but a place as far away in imagination as the Land of Oz.

Peary Caribou, 1991 (previous page)
Low Light – Willow Ptarmigan, 1995
Jimmy Emataluk – Inuit Guide, 1953

The arctic twilight was filled with the calls of birds, almost all of them unfamiliar to my southern Ontario ears: the guttural cluckings of ptarmigan, the wheedling whistles of whimbrel and the courtship songs of countless shorebirds that were busy going about the business of breeding. As my five companions and I watched our aircraft disappear into the fading light, we were acutely aware that we were quite possibly the first human

beings ever to walk there. The two "locals" in our party, Inuit men from nearby Leaf Bay, claimed that none of their people had ever ventured this far into the interior. Their lives and livelihoods were on the coast. And no Europeans had disturbed it—until a big mining company decided that iron ore might be profitably extracted from the region.

I look back now over the more than forty years that have elapsed since that summer with a sense of wonder and privilege. Few people on our increasingly crowded planet can say that they have explored a land for the first time, but that was exactly what we did—even naming the unnamed lakes. When I wasn't performing the paid part of my work, I was painting, sketching, observing and collecting, among other things, small mammal specimens for the Royal Ontario Museum. But even while working I was constantly making small and large discoveries: the heat-conserving properties of the densely packed plants of a tundra tussock, at the center of which the air can be many degrees warmer than the air above, or the fact that you can always spot a rough-legged hawk's cliffside nest because of the telltale colony of orange lichens fertilized by many generations of hawk droppings. One day, when investigating one of these orange "bull's-eyes" I discovered a nest of gray gyrfalcons almost ready to head out on their own.

Since that wonderful summer I've returned to the Arctic many times, first to help with biological fieldwork and later as a tourist. But I will never get enough of this awe-inspiring land, whose bleakness I find so beautiful and whose plants and animals have evolved such ingenious strategies for survival.

Ungava Camp, 1996
Young Snowy Owl, 1988

Arctic Cliff – White Wolves, 1991

NATURAL WORLDS

Robert Bateman 1990©

If you've ever visited an arctic water-fowl breeding colony in June, you have witnessed nature at its most intense. In the late 1970s I spent a couple of weeks assisting a biologist friend with fieldwork he was conducting on snow geese that breed in the salt marshes along the shore of La Pérouse Bay, near Churchill, Manitoba. The bay forms a part of the Hudson Bay Lowlands that is slated to become a national park. It is a flat wet area dotted with tundra ponds and laced with meandering, gently flowing streams. Our camp was in the distributary of the wide but shallow Mast River.

I had a wonderful time doing the nec-essary fieldwork, though I'm sure the job would not be to everyone's liking. Most of every day I spent in hip waders, sloshing through the clear, shallow, amber-colored water of the delta as I moved from islet to islet, checking the eggs in each nest. We wanted to band every gosling as soon as it was hatched so we would have the most complete and accurate information possi-ble as we followed it through its life.

I was often wet and cold but I loved being in this exuberant world absolutely teeming with life. Birds were singing on their territories, courting, feeding, breed-ing and hatching, seemingly all at once. I saw common eiders, Arctic terns, American wigeons, oldsquaws, red-necked phalaropes and parasitic jaegers.

Wide Horizon – Tundra Swans, 1990
Proud Swimmer – Snow Goose, 1986

Pacific loons were common nesters, and I even came across the occasional red-throated loon.

I understand that La Pérouse Bay is quite a different place these days. Because of the sharp rise in the North American snow goose population, there are now ten times more geese at La Pérouse, but this is far from a good-news story. As the goose numbers have gone up, many other species have become extremely rare in the area.

It seems that the North American snow geese have exceeded their natural population limits because of the increased food—from human agriculture—that is now available in their wintering areas. This population explosion has devastated the breeding habitats of the central and eastern Arctic, on which many other species also depend. Until now the loss of breeding habitat hasn't hit the snow goose because its own demographics have not yet caught

Eider Ducks in Flight, 1996
Pacific Loon and Cotton Grass, 1995

up with it. But as its breeding areas become poorer and poorer, a population crash seems inevitable.

A decline like this combined with bad weather might prove disastrous. Arctic nesters must pack all the activities of the breeding season into a very short time so that the young are strong enough to migrate south before freeze-up. Farther north, where the season is even shorter and less reliable, bad weather can play havoc with breeding. A late snowstorm or an early freeze can mean big drops in population. If favorable weather conditions don't appear for several years in a row, the declines in population can be precipitous.

It seems appropriate that a giant white bear should epitomize the Arctic, since the word *Arctic* comes from *arktikós*, the name the ancient Greeks gave to the constellation we call Ursa Major, the great bear. They called the land lying beneath this constellation "the country of the great bear." And so it has proved to be, though it is a very different country from the one they imagined: a region of rich soils and soft warm breezes. In fact, such a land would be most unfriendly to the polar bear, which is superbly adapted to the cold.

It may seem amazing that the world's largest carnivore lives in a land so harsh and unforgiving. Yet there is a natural logic to the bear's great size: it conserves heat. Relative to its total mass—the males can weigh almost two thousand pounds—the polar bear exposes proportionately much less surface area to those cold and sunless winter days than a collared lemming or an Arctic fox.

A mature polar bear is one of nature's most skilled and patient hunters. It will prey on almost any animal, but in winter its favorite food is seal—especially the ringed seal, the most abundant of the Arctic-dwelling seals. Like polar bears, ringed seals are solitary creatures. In winter they live under the ice, somehow finding their way back to their breathing

Arctic Landscape – Polar Bear, 1992

holes when they need a shot of oxygen.

When stalking a seal, polar bears may adopt several strategies, sometimes even pretending to be a chunk of ice drifting gradually toward an ice floe where a seal is hauled out for a breather. In winter, when open water is scarce or nonexistent, a bear may lie patiently for many hours beside a breathing hole, waiting for the seal to return. Sometimes it will even build a wall of snow and hide behind it. If its patience is rewarded, a brief gush of water will announce the seal's arrival. Then, in a single lightning-quick movement, the bear will pounce.

Just off Baffin Island during a recent cruise in the eastern Arctic with my entire extended family, we were able to get quite close to a polar bear that had recently caught a seal. As our ship approached through drifting floes, the bear regarded us warily but was clearly unwilling to give up its recent acquisition. When we neared the floe it was on, it jumped into the water and swam alongside the ship. Everyone on board crowded to the rails, certain that the bear would soon disappear. Instead, it climbed onto another floe and shook its prize in the air before finally diving back into the water and swimming away with seal in tow.

Polar Bear Portrait, 1992

Polar Bear Skull, 1991

Arctic Ice – Polar Bear, 1995 (overleaf)

Robert Bateman 1991

The
Eastern
Forest

I N FAIRY TALES FORESTS HAVE OFTEN BEEN DEPICTED AS DARK AND DANGEROUS PLACES. WHAT COULD BE MORE frightening to a small child than the thought of being lost in the woods, at the mercy of wolves or bears? For me, however, the forest has always been a place of fascination and mystery, never of fear. Throughout my life forests have been places of discovery and self-discovery.

My first forest was the ravine behind the house my father built when I was six. To my boyish eyes this small wooded valley through which a clear tributary of the Don River ran was an untamed wilderness—even though a steam engine puffed its way along the valley floor twice a day delivering coal and ice for the residents of North Toronto. It seemed as exotic as any tropical rainforest, this remnant of the rich and beautiful mixed forests of maple, beech, ash, pine and hemlock that had covered the area before the Europeans came. Because the ravine was wet, giant willows also flourished, as did a jungly undergrowth of fox grapes and Virginia creeper.

In spring the stream overflowed, leaving pools where tadpoles developed into frogs and painted turtles occasionally swam. Before the canopy leafed in, the forest floor was carpeted with wildflowers: trilliums, hepaticas, trout lilies and even lady slipper orchids. But best of all was the spring bird migration.

Toronto's ravines act as funnels concentrating great numbers of the birds that cross Lake Ontario each spring on their journey north. I vividly remember one sunny day in early May when I was perhaps ten or eleven sitting in a fragrant bower of wild plum blossoms, waiting to see what birds would come. Within the space of less than an hour I saw legions of warblers and kinglets, a yellow-bellied sapsucker and a ruby-throated hummingbird. At times it seemed as if every branch of every tree was dripping with birds.

Peregrine and Young, 1995 (previous page)
Bluebird and Blossoms, 1990
Prothonotary Warbler, 1994

As I grew older and found friends with similar interests, I ventured farther afield. The edge of the city was only a short bike ride away, and in no time

91

we found ourselves in a rolling countryside of fields and pastures interspersed with woodlots—a landscape providing a wonderful variety of bird habitats. Each time we spotted a new species we would come home elated. It was on one of these trips that I first saw a red-shouldered hawk. Although it was a fairly common bird in southern Ontario at the time, it was difficult to see except during migration because it nests and hunts in the high forest canopy.

A particular pleasure of early spring was a visit to a sugarbush, a maple woodlot being tapped to make maple syrup. The sap begins to run when temperatures exceed freezing during the day then drop below freezing at night. In fact, this alternation between freeze and thaw is crucial to a good flow. During my childhood, sap was still collected by traditional methods, in much the same way that native people had taught the early pioneers to harvest it. When the sap buckets were full, they were emptied into a gathering tank on a horse-drawn sled for transport to the sugar house, where the sap was evaporated in big pans over a constantly stoked wood fire.

When I recall maple-sugaring time, I hear the snorting of horses and feel the crunch of last year's leaves beneath the granular late-spring snow. The warm spring sun shines through a barren tracery of branches, casting filigree shadow patterns on the ground. I know that in a few weeks the woods will come alive with wildflowers, but the only signs of life for now are the running sap and perhaps an early returning migrant like a yellow-rumped warbler. Inside the sugar house acrid woodsmoke mixes with the sweet smell of maple vapors, reputed to be a sure-fire cure for a spring cold. Such memories evoke for me a simpler time, when communal labor was a regular part of most people's lives.

Sap Bucket – Myrtle Warbler, 1993
Backyard Birds, 1944
Spring Thaw – Red-tailed Hawk, 1993 (overleaf)

B efore my family and I moved to Canada's West Coast, our foothold on the planet was a property I bought in Halton County, southern Ontario, in 1959. I loved those ten sloping acres nestled in the Niagara Escarpment and the house I later designed and built there. In the 1960s the Escarpment was already the only rough country that remained in the environs of Metropolitan Toronto, which is why I moved there. From my studio window I had a splendid view of one of the Escarpment's more impressive eminences, Rattlesnake Point.

I contemplated that view in every weather and every season, by day and by night. But probably my favorite time was during those golden days of autumn when the eastern hardwood forest is at its most exuberant. My daily hike through our woods and meadow was a feast for the senses. I reveled in the rich dank smell of decay and the incredible variety of form and color— the jewelweed and goldenrod that often grew as high as my chin and the intricate tracery of wild grapes, whose leaves, stems and tendrils remind me of Tiffany lamps.

On a corner of my property in Halton County I planted a stand of white pines from little seedlings. The white pine has long been one of my favorite trees, particularly because of the soft billowy effect created by its feathery foliage. This was a favorite playground for my children Alan, John and Sarah, and, later, Christopher and Robbie.

A decade or so after I planted those trees, a neighbor asked me if he could place some of his beehives in my white pine stand. The trees provided shade for the hives, and in the nearby meadow there was summer nectar for the bees. The bargain worked out well. At the end of each year the beekeeper gave our family a bucket of excellent honey as payment.

In late fall, when the bees became dormant, our neighbor came and wrapped the hives in tarpaper to protect them from the cold. That's how I remember them now, surrounded by snow and lit by the ruddy glow of a winter sunset.

Fox and Beehives, 1995
Fox Etching, 1985
The Scolding – Chickadees and Screech Owl,
1990 (overleaf)

THE EASTERN FOREST

Owls have long been creatures of myth and mystery. The ancient Greeks associated them with Athena, the goddess of wisdom—hence the expression "wise as an owl." In other cultures they have been held in awe or viewed with fear. Sometimes they are seen as heralds of victory or harbingers of good luck; at other times they are thought of as ill omens foretelling disaster. The aura of mystery surrounding owls is heightened by two of their characteristics: the fringed feathers at the ends of their wings allow them to fly almost soundlessly, and, with a few exceptions, they are nocturnal and therefore often very difficult to see.

The largest of our owls, the great horned owl, is a creature of the dark night and the deep forest who nests up high, usually in an abandoned hawk's nest or in a tree cavity. I have spent many hours searching for this fierce hunter, which will catch and eat birds as large as a small goose and mammals as fleet as the snowshoe hare. It also dines on porcupine and skunk. If I'm lucky, a noisy mob of crows will lead me to its roost. Crows, which dislike all owls, find great horned owls especially reprehensible. (They have good reason for this, since by night crows become one of this owl's prey.) If they find a great horned owl trying to take a nap, they will scold it relentlessly.

Another method for locating an owl is to look for pellets on the forest floor. Because owls have no crop, they can't digest the bones and fur of the birds and small mammals they consume; these are regurgitated in the form of sausage-shaped pellets that provide wildlife biologists with wonderful information about owl diets. If you find pellets beneath a tree, there's a good chance that somewhere above an owl will be sleeping.

Winter Pine – Great Horned Owl, 1993
White on White – Snowshoe Hare, 1988
Winter Companion – Yellow Labrador, 1985 (overleaf)

To residents of southern Ontario, the term "cottage" means a simple summer place, ideally situated by a rockbound lake and surrounded by a forest wilderness. But in my late teens my family began visiting our Haliburton, Ontario, cottage in winter. Our first attempt wasn't too encouraging, since we couldn't get the stove to draw properly and so had to keep all the windows open when we were cooking. (Only when we returned the next summer did we discover that a mouse had built a nest in the chimney.) After this first visit, however, we came to love our winter escapes from the city. A constant fire kept our cabin warm and cosy, and it was no great hardship to transport water from a hole chopped in the ice of the nearby lake.

Almost every day my brothers and I set out to explore a different route, sometimes following established trails and sometimes breaking new ones through the bush. Next to canoeing, snowshoeing and cross-country skiing have long been my favorite forms of wilderness travel. Both are faster than walking, especially if you're traveling along the flat edges of lakes or rivers.

Everywhere the snow altered the landscape, and turned familiar objects into simplified sculptural forms. Even the wooden chair my father liked to sit in and the picnic table where we often ate on summer days were transformed into wonderful works of found art.

Cottage at Lake Boshkung – Winter, 1996
Picnic Table – Pileated Woodpeckers, 1987

108

Robert Bateman 1987

Morning Cove – Common Loon, 1988
Rocky Point, October, 1987

As a boy at my parents' cottage, canoeing became one of my great loves. To this day, the classic canvas-covered cedar-strip canoe conjures up those summers at the lake more than any other image. After all, the canoe's two basic building materials—cedar and canvas—were common elements of our daily lives away from the city. Rot-resistant eastern white cedar made excellent lumber for building cottages, and canvas made sturdy clothes as well as tents in those days before the invention of synthetics. It was at the cottage that I learned to paddle with a dripless stroke for maximum stealth, never removing the blade from the water and being careful not to bump the gunwale.

Much as I love hiking, to me the perfect way to experience the wilderness is by canoe. Paddling quietly down a winding river or along a lakeshore, you can get much closer to wildlife than on a woodland trail. As I grew older, the canoe also connected me to the painters I began to emulate, the expert woodsmen and canoeists of the Group of Seven, who often paddled to their painting sites. Like them I often worked outdoors—a habit that I discovered can have unanticipated side effects: the canvases from my late teens preserve hundreds, possibly thousands, of mosquitoes that committed suicide on their still-gooey surfaces.

Robert Bateman 1987©

From year to year bird populations can vary substantially, but this is not necessarily a cause for alarm. The wide fluctuations in the numbers of Cape May warblers, for example, seem to follow the population cycles of the spruce budworm on which they feed. However, some familiar birds of my youth have suffered declines that seem to be long-term and are therefore much more worrisome. These days you almost never hear the beautiful, bell-like, three-syllable song of the wood thrush during a walk through the deep forests it loves. And both the brown thrasher and the rufous-sided towhee that visited my backyard ravine when I was a boy are seen much less frequently now.

The reasons for such declines are not always clear. In some cases, loss of breeding habitat is the obvious cause. In Ontario, the prothonatory warbler has lost so much breeding ground that there may

be no more than ten pairs left. The fragmentation of forests is certainly partly to blame as well, as is the use of chemical pesticides. Another cause is tropical deforestation. Bachman's warbler has vanished from its former breeding range in the southeastern United States, for example, because the Cuban forests where this bird wintered have virtually disappeared to make way for sugar cane plantations.

One autumn not long ago, I came across an ovenbird lying on the forest floor, dead of unknown causes. There was no sign that it had been attacked by a predator, yet there it lay, a hauntingly beautiful still life. In my mind it came to represent the disquieting decline of bird populations worldwide.

Fall – Ovenbird, 1991
Cape May Warbler and Balsam, 1992
Mangrove Shadow – Common Egret,
1991 (overleaf)

Robert Bateman 1992

Like many eastern Canadian birds, a large number of Canada's human inhabitants migrate to Florida each winter. While my personal migrations are less predictable, they do periodically take me into this subtropical realm. But most often these days my trips to Florida are spent visiting my print publisher, Mill Pond Press, in Venice.

After a long day I generally take an evening walk. It was on one such stroll a few years ago that I came across the old Venice train station, abandoned and derelict. Its grandiose Romanesque arches are now defaced with graffiti and a super-highway roars overhead, but I like to imagine it in its heyday in the 1920s when trains were the only sensible way to travel long distances.

Egrets regularly feed in a canal that runs nearby, and I recalled that these birds were once as endangered as the passenger train is today. In the nineteenth century they were brutally hunted for their plumes, which were much coveted for fashionable ladies' hats. Sometimes the hunters would rip the plumes out of a living bird and leave it to a slow and agonizing death. In fact, the creation of the Audubon Society was spurred by a group of blue-blooded Boston ladies who were outraged by this barbaric practice. Thus the egret in my painting of the train station faces north, toward Boston, the birthplace of one of the great forces for wildlife conservation in North America.

Venice Train Station, 1991
Great Egret Preening, 1986

117

Robert Bateman 1991 ©

M any people's idea of paradise is a sandy beach, sparkling blue water and a cloudless sky. Although I am more drawn to rocky shores and foggy days, I am not immune to the joys of sun and sand and laughing gulls wheeling overhead. And as a birder, I delight in the profusion of shorebirds that feed along Florida beaches in the wintertime. But paradise usually comes with a price tag. Tucked under one of the chairs in the painting is a bit of conscious symbolism, a half-empty can of diet soda. Like so much of North American culture, the contents of the can are sweet and fizzy, but artificially made and empty of nutritional value.

Gulf Coast – Laughing Gulls, 1991
Egret and Full Moon, 1991

The
Tropics

Robert Bateman 1994

O N A RECENT TRIP TO CENTRAL AMERICA MY FAMILY SPENT several days living with a traditional Kekchi Mayan farm family in southern Belize. Though their life was simple, almost devoid of the modern gadgets we take for granted, it seemed very satisfactory to me. They lived in a palm-thatched house without electricity but with abundant natural air conditioning. Everything we ate during our visit was raised or grown on the family farm or came from the surrounding forest. After dinner, as we sat around the coal-oil lamp and asked our hosts about their lives, what came across most strongly to me was their sense of dignity and self-respect.

The Mayans have been agricultural people for as long as anyone can remember. In fact, some archaeologists attribute the rapid decline of the pre-Columbian Mayan civilization to a crash in agricultural productivity, possibly triggered by a climate change resulting from widespread deforestation. But the modern-day Mayans of the Yucatán Peninsula, of which Belize is a part, practice a sustainable form of agriculture that does not threaten the forest. My hosts carefully rotate crops of corn, beans and rice, leaving some fields fallow to allow the soil to regenerate. This forms an instructive contrast to the slash-and-burn agriculture typical of much of the American tropics, where the soils of the freshly felled forest are quickly exhausted and the farms abandoned.

Walking through the soft green twilight of a mature Central American rainforest, you would never guess it could be so fragile. Great columnlike trunks, many of them with enormous natural buttresses, disappear into the dense green canopy. The trees are often festooned with epiphytic plants—ferns, mosses, orchids, bromeliads and cacti—which draw their moisture from the air. Giant lianas climb skyward, using the trees as trellises to reach the sun. The warm

King Vulture, 1995 (previous page)
Mayan and Hut, 1994
Chiclero, 1994

123

humid air is heavy with the perfumes of flowers and decaying plant matter, and it is often filled with insects, including legions of colorful butterflies. But most of the action is in the canopy, where troops of howler monkeys and flocks of foraging birds pass noisily overhead and the three-toed sloth hangs upside down, munching contentedly.

An old *chiclero*, who had formerly made his living harvesting the viscous sap of the chicle tree, once the main constituent of chewing gum, was our guide one day in the Maya Mountains of southwestern Belize. As he led us through the forest, he pointed out the trees to avoid—like the black poisonwood, whose sap will cause an acute rash more serious than the effects of poison ivy. Fortunately, the antidote for poisonwood, the gumbo limbo tree, often grows nearby, its russet-colored bark resembling scaly, burnt skin.

As we ascended a long slope, the dense broadleafed jungle gave way to the airy pine forest that occupies the higher slopes. Suddenly we came out onto the brink of a spectacular gorge with a waterfall plunging dramatically in the distance. We trained our binoculars and telescopes on the exposed rocks to discover a flock of roosting king vultures, the rarest and most beautiful member of this family. While we watched, some of the vultures launched themselves into the great open space between us. Some rode the air currents until they circled directly over our heads.

So vast and diverse is the tropical rainforest that it remains a mostly undiscovered country whose sheer genetic diversity is one of the most powerful arguments for preserving as much of it as possible. Although tropical forests now cover less than 6 percent of the earth's land surface, they harbor more than half of all living species. Many modern medicines have been derived from rainforest species and the cure for cancer may well be hiding in the cells of some still-to-be-discovered plant or animal. Furthermore, sustainably managed tropical forests can yield a vast number of useful products: oils, resins, fruits, nuts and fibers.

I believe that one of the keys to saving tropical forests from extinction is to support the struggle of forest-dwelling people to claim ownership of their land and to gain control over how it is used. They will be its wisest stewards.

Under the Canopy – Keel-billed Toucan, 1994
Symbol of the Rainforest – Spotted Jaguar,
1994 (overleaf)

Robert Bateman 1994©

L ike the leopard, the ocelot cannot change its spots, and this is the source of its current misfortune. The ocelot's elegant markings make its pelt much prized for fur coats, and though it is shy and agile, it is relatively easy to trap. Despite international efforts to protect it and other spotted cats, the ocelot is in danger of being hunted to extinction. Before its fur came into fashion, however, the ocelot's spots served it well, providing perfect camouflage in forest habitats characterized by dappled sun and shade.

Reclining Ocelot, 1994

Sitting Ocelot, 1995

On our trip to Costa Rica's Monteverde Cloud Forest Reserve, we followed a trail that took us to a vantage point overlooking a forest valley. Ragged clouds and mist hung in the highland hollows, highlighting the contours of the landscape, but the sky above us was clear. And into that clear sky swooped a pair of the most elegant of all birds of prey, the swallow-tailed kite—a creature I'd dreamed of seeing ever since I was a boy.

My wife, Birgit, is often the first in any group to spot an elusive rarity. And she was the first among us to discern the perched figure of a resplendent quetzal, its emerald-green feathers blending into the dense foliage across the valley. Soon we all had this most famous member of the trogon family in our sights. It was my first look at the sacred bird of the Aztecs, whose kings and nobles wore the bird's long upper-tail coverts in their elaborate headdresses. The quetzal sat perfectly still and upright on its perch. Then it slowly turned its head as if to look at us, its large eyes more mild than wild, yet its face somehow embodying the spirit of the deep mysterious tropical forest.

Quetzal, 1993

Rainforest – Swallow-tailed Kite, 1994

Part of my fascination with the jaguar, the largest wild cat of the Americas, stems from my interest in big predators. But like many large carnivores that live at the peak of their particular food pyramid, the jaguar also stands as a symbol of the disappearing tropical forest. Its varied diet alone demonstrates the diversity of the habitat it requires, preying as it does on at least sixty different species, including the razor-tusked rainforest pig called the peccary, and the capybara, which as the largest living rodent weighs as much as 132 pounds.

I've never seen a jaguar in the wild—only jaguar footprints in the jungles of Belize. But that somehow seems appropriate for this swift and solitary hunter. The jaguar once ranged from the southwestern United States to southern Argentina. Now, except in the still-vast rainforest of the Amazon basin, jaguars are very rare, their numbers having been drastically reduced by big-game hunters and vanishing habitat.

Even if we manage to set aside a few forest reserves to protect the jaguar, in the long run that won't be enough. When wild habitats become isolated from each other, they begin to lose their biological diversity. Smaller islands of habitat present an even greater problem, since some wide-ranging species simply may not have enough ground to cover. And in protected

Shadow of the Rainforest – Black Jaguar, 1992

133

preserves species that have adapted to the human presence soon become dominant, while their isolated wild cousins fall prey to inbreeding.

That's the reason I've recently lent support to Wildlife Conservation International's initiative, Paseo Pantera, the Path of the Panther. The dream behind this scheme is a continuous natural corridor from Panama to the U.S.-Mexican border, along which a single panther could theoretically travel. Such a corridor would help ensure the survival of the big cats and the species-rich forests in which they thrive. But I see no reason why this scheme should not be extended to aim for something grander, perhaps a natural pathway from Tierra del Fuego to the Yukon. The panther, also known as the puma, cougar or mountain lion, can still be found throughout this enormous range and can live in almost every natural habitat from desert to tropical forest.

Path of the Panther, 1993

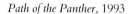

Robert Bateman 1994©

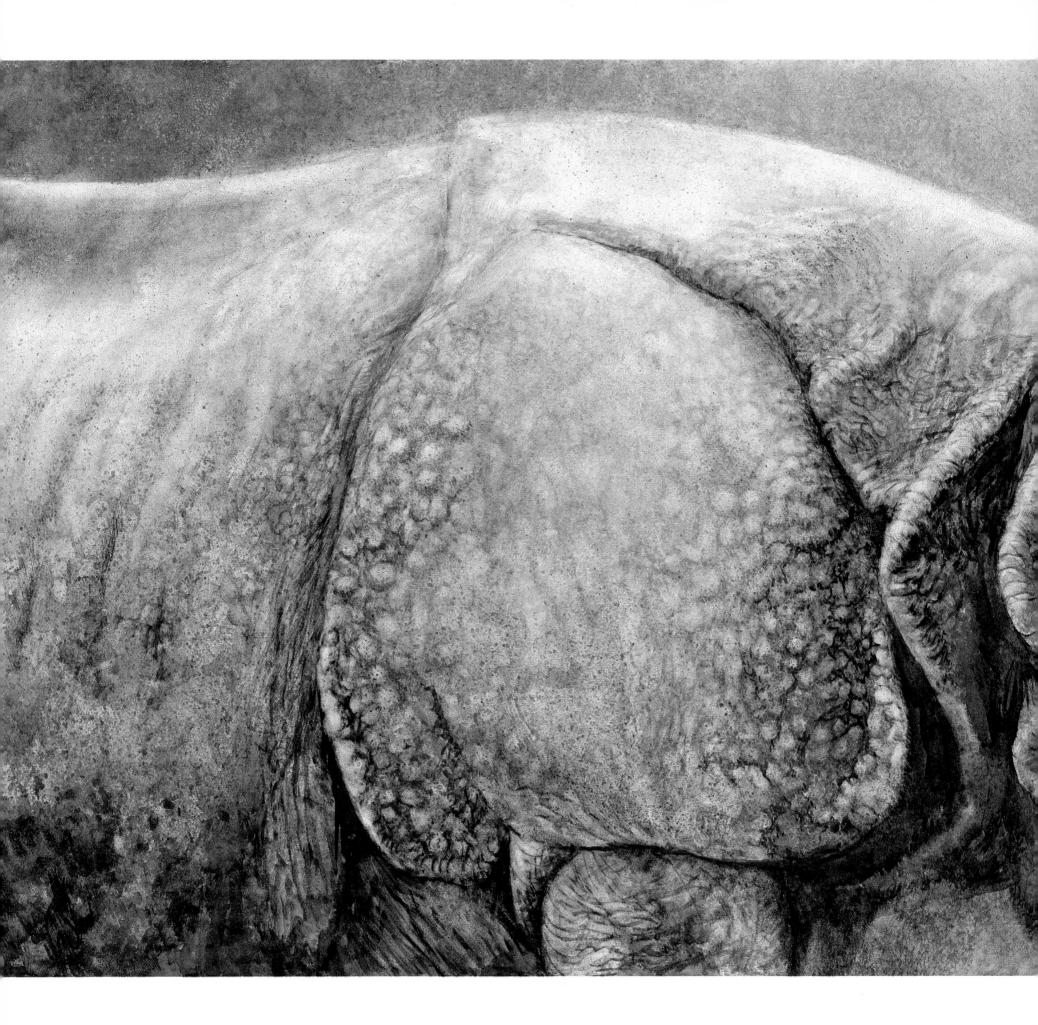

Old
Worlds

A<small>S A BOY TURNING THE</small> pages of the *National Geographic*, I traveled in my imagination to the far corners of the earth, gaining my first taste for the extraordinary diversity of natural environments and human cultures on our planet. As I grew older and began to make my own journeys, my appetite for the

earth's variety only increased. As much as I revel in my own backyard, I still can't resist the temptation to explore the new and the unknown.

More often than not, my favorite places are those where I've actually spent enough time to feel at home, places I've either lived in or explored more than once. I've often said that I take great pleasure in repeatedly walking particular paths, observing the subtle changes from day to day and from season to season. Likewise, only when a foreign place becomes familiar does it yield up its secrets. Still, there is no denying the thrill of love at first sight, and I continue to be drawn to places I've never visited and will probably never see again.

Of all my travels, by far the greatest adventure was my trip around the world in 1957-58. I was in my late twenties, not yet married, and I jumped at the idea when my friend Bristol Foster proposed it. Bristol and I planned our itinerary one Sunday afternoon with nothing more than a high school atlas. We had no idea what we were getting into. But I now look back at our circumnavigation of the globe by ship and Land Rover as one of the mountain peaks of my life.

Our route took us across equatorial Africa, by ship to Bombay, then by

Indian Rhinoceros, 1995 (previous page)
Sumatran Tiger, 1995
Land Rover Campsite in Bamboo, 1958

land into Nepal and Sikkim (where we met the crown prince). After considerable negotiation we had the rare good fortune of obtaining permission to drive through Burma to Thailand and Malaysia. From Singapore we headed to northwestern Australia, then drove across the interior desert to the coast and boarded a ship for Vancouver. We were home in Toronto by Christmas 1958, about eighteen months after departing.

Wherever we went, we soaked up everything we could about the locality, its anthropology and art, its botany, biology and geology. When I think of this wonderful time, my mind is crowded with competing images. Among the most vivid was my first experience of the extraordinary megafauna of the East African game reserves. Perhaps our most physically challenging and biologically fascinating adventure came when we climbed the fabled Mountains of the Moon on the Uganda-Zaire border. We began in equatorial rainforest and ended in a region of permanent snowfields and glaciers more than sixteen thousand feet above sea level. And unquestionably one of the highlights of the entire trip was our sojourn with the Ba Mbuti pygmies in the equatorial rainforest of what was then the Belgian Congo. These traditional hunter-gatherers had an amazing knowledge of their jungle world and constantly expressed the joy of their close relationship with it. All their songs were hymns of praise to the forest and its bounty. Nor will I ever forget our stay in the Cameron Highlands of Malaysia with the Senoi people. These forest dwellers lived in perfect harmony with nature, but even in the 1950s their old world was disappearing as the authorities tried to educate them in twentieth-century ways. Now their forests have been "harvested" and their sophisticated knowledge of forest ecosystems has been lost.

I returned from this trip with a new sense of self-confidence, but more important, a new-found appreciation of difference. I had filled my sketchbooks with drawings of plants and animals, people and objects I could not previously have imagined. And I came to the conclusion that the cliché "We're all the same under the skin" is incorrect. Each of us is different in important ways that are to be celebrated and cherished. Each distinct culture is as precious as a unique natural ecosystem. Variety is not just the spice of life, it is the essence of life.

Ba Mbuti Pygmies, 1958
Malaysian Aboriginal, 1996
Senoi Huts, 1958

Nothing could be more modern, more urban, more high-tech than a city like Tokyo. Yet what surprised me more than anything on my first trip to Japan was how the twentieth-century landscape coexists with a much older and more traditional landscape and culture in what appears to be harmony.

Riding the bullet train from Tokyo to Kyoto, I looked out the window on a pastoral scene that is little different from the one that existed several hundred years ago: fields and forests as far as the eye can see. And during my visit to an old garden in the ancient imperial capital I watched as a businessman checked his briefcase at the gate, then sat and quietly meditated just as a Samurai knight of the seventeenth century might have done.

Although Japanese business is sometimes criticized for its conservation attitudes, Japan has looked after its own environment quite well. For example, it has done a much better job of preserving its forests than most developed countries: more than half its total land area is woodland. One of the highlights of my first trip was a visit to a wonderful forest reserve on

Macaque Family, 1995

Tokyo Pond – Spotbilled Ducks, 1995

the mountainous volcanic island of Yakushima off the south coast. The reserve protects ancient Japanese red cedars, one of which is more than three thousand years old, along with a population of sacred macaques, short-tailed Asian monkeys. Increasingly, the Japanese are establishing parks and reserves to protect threatened habitats and species. Even the rare red-crowned crane, which almost disappeared in the 1950s, has made a comeback.

The recovery of the red-crowned crane demonstrates the deep connection ordinary Japanese people feel to nature, a connection that undoubtedly derives in part from the Shinto religion with its deep reverence for the natural world. When the crane's plight became known, it caused national concern. Because it mates for life and lives more than fifty years, this bird has come to symbolize happiness, marital fidelity and long life. Now its future seems reasonably secure.

Cries of Courtship – Red-crowned Cranes, 1991
Old Willow – Mandarin Pair, 1995 (overleaf)

145

Robert Bateman 1985 ©

On my visit to the Wolong Nature Preserve in China's Sichuan Province, I hoped against hope that I might actually catch a glimpse of one of the world's wildlife celebrities, the giant panda. But it was not to be. Except during breeding season, pandas avoid all company, even that of their own kind. And despite their strong white and black coloring, they quickly disappear into the dense undergrowth.

The panda's habitat, however, made me feel right at home. As we climbed the narrow switchback trail that had begun in neatly terraced fields, we entered a region of huge old-growth trees covered with snow that had fallen the previous night. (The pandas depend on these old trees for dens.) Many of the tree species—pine, fir, hemlock, larch and birch—were familiar, as was the cool misty weather. Except for the dense bamboo thickets, I could almost have been walking in an old-growth forest of the Pacific Northwest.

But above all, it is the bamboo understory that makes these mountain habitats the place for pandas. They feed almost exclusively on this difficult-to-digest and nutrient-poor plant. As descendents of the ancient carnivore ancestor of modern bears, pandas lack the digestive adaptations that might allow them to use their plant food to the maximum, and so they compensate by eating constantly and digesting quickly, on average eighteen pounds a day. To conserve energy, they generally sleep whenever they're not eating, but this still leaves them close to the edge of malnutrition. When a species of bamboo suddenly flowers and dies off—as it may do once in many years—the panda population can drop catastrophically. This is a particular problem now that the lower slopes, where different bamboo species provided an alternate food source, have been cleared by logging.

Despite all the attention the panda has been getting these past few years, its situation is far from promising. The Chinese authorities seem more interested in raising pandas in captivity and sending them on highly publicized foreign tours than in taking the difficult steps needed to save and restore their habitat. The birth of a captive panda in the Wolong Nature Preserve is a great photo opportunity that gets worldwide coverage. Meanwhile little progress is being made in eliminating poaching, returning the cleared lower slopes to forest, replanting lower-altitude bamboo species, and most important of all, linking the increasingly isolated panda reserves by protected natural corridors.

Pandas at Play, 1988
Giant Panda in the Wild, 1993
Winter Filigree – Giant Panda, 1995 (overleaf)

Robert Bateman—1993©

On my trips to India and Asia I've seen a wild tiger just once, during a visit to the Kaziranga Wildlife Reserve in the state of Assam in northeastern India. This reserve also harbors a wild population of Indian elephants and rare one-horned rhinos. One afternoon while birdwatching in a marshy area of the reserve, we spotted a herd of marsh deer browsing peacefully among the grass and sedges across a stretch of open water from where we were standing. Suddenly the deer all turned their heads to look back over their shoulders. With my binoculars I followed their gaze until a tawny orange shape appeared in my field of vision: a Bengal tiger. Not realizing his prey had been alerted, he continued his stealthy approach. Then he charged, crashing through the water. By the time he reached his target, however, the deer were gone. He stood for a few minutes in the clearing, bathed in the late afternoon sunlight, then disappeared into the thickets. It was a rare look at one of the rarest wild animals on earth.

Snowy Nap – Tiger, 1993

Siberian Tiger, 1991

Sudden Move – Siberian Tiger, 1995 (overleaf)

Of all the places I visited during my trip around the world, none made a deeper impression on me than East Africa. The great game reserves of Kenya and Tanzania were even more astonishing than I had imagined, with their vast migrating herds of zebra and wildebeest, their roaming bands of elephant, giraffe and buffalo, and their magnificent predators: leopards, cheetahs and lions. I have stood on a hill overlooking the Serengeti Plain and seen herds of antelope and zebra stretching as far as the eye could see. There is nothing like these places left anywhere else on earth. Each time I return—and I have returned many times—I feel as though I am being transported a million years back in time to the Pleistocene, when our early ancestors were still emerging from the evolutionary murk, into a thrilling encounter with primordial nature.

Tembo, 1990
Baby Elephant Drawing, 1988

157

African Amber – Lioness Pair, 1977

Passing Fancy – Lion Cubs and Rhino, 1992

The sisterhood of lionesses ranks as one of the greatest relationships among females that I have observed in the natural world. And no wildlife experience surpasses watching a group of lionesses engaged in a hunt. This usually happens in the hour or two before dusk when the light of late afternoon makes their tawny coats glow like amber among the golden grasses. When the prey is spotted, each lioness enters a state of supreme alertness: she becomes a total hunting being. And yet somehow, perhaps by a form of telepathy, the group communicates, often carrying out quite a sophisticated strategy. I've seen a lioness team deliberately lay a trap whereby two or three will lie downwind of the unsuspecting prey while the others move in from upwind, driving their dinner into the clutches of their companions.

Contrary to popular perception, a lion kill is seldom gory. First the prey is knocked down, then the attacker positions herself on its back in order to avoid a damaging hoof kick. (For a lion, a broken jaw means certain slow starvation.) She then suffocates her prey, often by grabbing its entire muzzle in her mouth, then stretching the neck with her forelegs and turning the head back and up. For the next few minutes there is a life-and-death struggle at the end of which the lioness may well be too exhausted to enjoy her success.

This is when the male usually shows up. A lioness may bluff a defense against his invasion, but in the end she usually lets the male lion take his share.

Dispute Over Prey, 1975

The final day of our family's visit to Zaire's Kahuzi-Biega National Park turned out to be the lucky one. After clambering for several hours along slippery hilly trails through dense undergrowth and occasional stinging nettles, we found a feeding troop of eastern lowland gorillas. The troop not only tolerated our presence but allowed us to join them for their after-dinner rest hour.

Some of the gorillas were sleeping in the shade at the edge of the clearing; others were grooming themselves. One baby played with its mother's hand, tiny fingers against giant ones. The big dignified silverback—mature males can be identified by the silvery gray hair on their backs—was the troop leader. He sat in the sun, apparently dozing, but in fact aware of everyone within his extended family. The sense of harmony and domesticity these animals displayed gave me a feeling of great mellowness and calm.

We lay down at the clearing's edge, pretending that we too were resting, and

waited. Soon curiosity got the better of some of the gorilla adolescents. First one and then another rolled and stretched, then somersaulted in our direction, gradually working their way closer to where we lay. Finally, one of these teenagers got close enough to reach out toward my outstretched hand. But just before our fingers touched, the old silverback grunted sharply and the young gorilla somersaulted back to a satisfactory distance. For that one moment, however, human and gorilla almost met.

In retrospect, I realize that however magical that touch might have been, it was just as well it was prevented. Who knows what a human disease might do to an ape lacking our particular immune defenses? Still, the image of a hand reaching across the unimaginable gap between two species will remain with me always.

Pensive Moment – Juvenile Gorilla, 1995
Intrusion – Mountain Gorilla, 1992

NATURAL WORLDS

Much has been written about how the Israelis have made the desert bloom, rendering fertile what was once a barren land. Less well known is their dedication to nature conservation, a tricky endeavor in such a tiny crowded country where the demands of the military and the pressures for development are immense. Yet Israel has managed to set aside 23 percent of its total land area as protected nature reserves. And their Nature Reserves Authority is dedicated to nothing short of restoring the flora and fauna of the Old Testament to its former habitats.

The record so far is one of remarkable success. By 1963, the year the Reserves Authority was created, most of the beasts of the Bible had disappeared or were on the verge of extinction. Since then, forests have been replanted and many animals roam once more in the wild, among them the onager (the biblical wild ass), the wild boar, the desert gazelle, the Nubian ibex, and several predators, including the desert leopard and the wolf. The return of these two large carnivores strikes me as truly remarkable in a world that until recently seemed dedicated to extinguishing all major land predators.

I came away from my visit to Israel convinced that it is one of the most conservation-conscious countries in the world. When military aircraft were found to be interfering with some of the millions of birds that use the skies over Israel during migration, a study was performed to time training flights so they would be least disruptive. Every Israeli schoolchild must spend time in nature education, and a million students visit the nature reserves each year. And army officers, whose troops often perform maneuvers in protected areas, must be trained as naturalists.

Israeli Leopard, 1995
Ibex at Masada Study, 1996

Stork and Well, Sieburczyn, 1992
Polish Stableyard, 1993

I am a fervent supporter of wilderness protection for ecological, ethical, aesthetic and spiritual reasons. But I am equally devoted to the preservation of places where human beings have altered nature without diminishing it, developing complex ecosystems in which *Homo sapiens* plays an essential part. In such ancient cultural landscapes, as they are aptly called, to take away the human element would be to diminish ecological diversity.

Small wonder, then, that I eagerly accepted the invitation of the Artists for Nature Foundation to spend two weeks in a remote village in northeastern Poland in the early spring of 1992. I was one of thirty-two artists from around the world who had gathered to paint and sketch the area and publicize the need for preserving it. The farmlands surrounding the village and the nearby wetlands along the Narew and Biebrza rivers—one of the last remaining lowland marshes in Europe—have evolved into one harmonious whole.

Except for a few cars and trucks and the occasional tractor, this is a world that operates in ways that have changed little for hundreds of years. Water is still drawn from wells by bucket. Low-lying fields—too soggy to bear a tractor's weight—are still cultivated by horse-drawn plows. Because chemical fertilizers and pesticides have been too expensive for the farmers and because the marshes have not been drained, the wildlife is varied and abundant. White storks can still be seen nesting on the thatched roofs of ancient barns. And

in winter, horsedrawn carts venture deep into the frozen marsh to collect sedges for winter fodder.

Picturesque, quaint, idyllic? Yes. But I believe we have to move beyond such words to understand the true value of places such as this. These people have retained and refined the art of living in a fine balance with their natural surroundings. And they know what it is to perform meaningful work, something that seems to have vanished for so many of us. They may be poor in the material sense but they feel a deep connection to the world in which they live.

Areas where traditional, sustainable agriculture is an essential element in a rich and complex natural tapestry are increasingly rare. One of the largest of such areas still remaining in Europe is found in the Spanish province of Extremadura. Here the next gathering of artists under the auspices of Artists for Nature took place in 1994. Lying to the south and east of Madrid, Extremadura is a region of forested mountains, rolling grasslands and open parkland. It is famous among naturalists as the main European wintering area of the Eurasian crane, fifty thousand of which arrive each year from scattered breeding grounds in Scandinavia.

But the cranes wouldn't be there if human beings hadn't altered the landscape thousands of years ago, partially clearing the original forest to create a parkland area known as the *dehesa*. The cranes depend on the acorns of the *dehesa*'s trees—holm oak and cork oak—for their primary winter

fodder. The regularly pruned oaks provide leaves for animal food and wood to be made into charcoal. The effect of the landscape is strange, almost artificial, with the loosely spaced, sculptured oaks stretching as far as you can see.

Among the animals that forage beneath these trees are the local free-range pigs, who fatten up on the same acorns that attract the cranes. In fact, over time the oaks have been selectively bred in favor of the sweetest nuts, which give Extremadura

ham its much-prized sweet flavor. Even though these pigs ultimately meet the same fate as their more confined relatives, they have a wonderful life while it lasts, bathing in crystal clear streams and browsing at will. One particular pig I got to know was owned by the proprietors of a two-thousand-year-old tavern, one of the oldest in Europe, which stands on an ancient Roman road and has been serving customers continuously since Roman times.

Spanish Pig, 1995

Stone Curlew and Rock, 1994

OLD WORLDS

Because my ancestors came from the British Isles, my visits there have always had a special resonance. Long before I saw an Irish cottage or a Scottish castle, I had been raised on a rich diet of English literature that gave such places a reality in my imagination.

This helps explain why my first visit to the village of Great Durnford in Wiltshire was particularly memorable. As I walked under the big old beeches that shaded the river, I felt as though I'd stepped into the pages of *The Wind in the Willows*. The pale white barn owl I glimpsed through the open door of the old Saxon church might have been a ghost from the time of *Beowulf*.

It was a world both familiar and strange. The weathered granary I painted reminded me of an old Ontario barn, and the red foxes in the neighborhood belonged to the same species I knew from home. But I'd never seen anything like the granary's unusual carved stone supports, whose mushroom shape was designed to prevent rats from raiding the stored grain.

Fox at the Granary, 1975

When it comes to finding a balance between progress and preservation, probably the best model we have is Western Europe. On my many visits there over the years, I've been increasingly impressed by the degree to which traditional landscapes and natural areas are appreciated and protected. If some parts of the world are still in their infancy in terms of looking after the environment, and we in North America are probably at the adolescent stage, then the Western Europeans are showing signs of having grown into responsible adults.

One aspect of this maturity is a willingness to accept limits on personal freedom in return for the trinity of "health, beauty and permanence" identified by E. F. Schumacher in his landmark book *Small Is Beautiful*. In general, environmental standards in Western Europe are much stricter than in North America, and despite a much denser population, there is no shortage of green space. While there are ugly alienating suburbs in some of the big cities, the countryside remains remarkably intact and strict rules generally require that new buildings blend in with the old. The view from the house in southern Germany where Birgit and I and our two boys lived for a year had hardly changed from the days of Mozart.

In Western Europe I see the beginning of the kind of shift in values that we are all going to have to make if we hope to restore and preserve true quality of life.

Country Lane – Pheasant, 1979
Backlight – Mute Swan, 1989

173

Red Grouse in Grass, 1994

Little Owl on Stone Fence, 1994

174

OLD WORLDS

Legacy

THE BIRTHS OF MY FIRST TWO GRANDCHILDREN WHILE THIS BOOK WAS BEING PREPARED FOR PRESS TURNED MY thoughts to the legacy of my own grandfather. In recent years I've gone back several times to his farm in eastern Ontario where my father grew up. Originally, several Bateman brothers lived and farmed side by side, and while Batemans no longer live on grandad's spread, the original house and barn are still standing and the property next door remains in the family. The farm is owned and actively farmed by my father's cousin Wilbur, his son and his grandchildren. Visiting them allows me to touch my roots among the Irish Protestant immigrants who cleared and settled much of southern Ontario in the mid-nineteenth century.

When I walk down the lane that marks the dividing line between the land owned by my grandfather and the land his brother (Wilbur's father) owned, I am aware of being in a place that, on the surface at least, hasn't changed much in more than a century. The stone fence that lines the lane stands as a kind of monument to those hard-working pioneers. It is humbling to realize how much sheer labor went into clearing the stones from the surrounding fields and building that fence in an age before engine-powered machinery. Yet the fence now seems as natural to the landscape as the plowed fields, the meadows and the woodlots.

My Bateman relatives are devoted to the land and determined to keep their farm a going concern, but they face increasingly long odds. The North American family farm is as much an endangered species as the Siberian tiger or the giant panda. That wouldn't worry me so much if we were replacing it with something better, but we're not. The industrial agriculture that replaces these farms substitutes sameness for variety and requires ever-increasing and more costly pollution-causing inputs in the forms of energy, chemical fertilizers and pesticides.

My grandfather's farm represents a piece of human heritage as valuable to me as any piece of wild nature. At its best, the rural landscape of Ontario resembles other places I've spoken of in this book where human beings have learned to live in harmony with nature, where something vital would be lost if the

Grandfather's Farm and Groundhog,
1995 (previous page)
At the Bridge – Cliff Swallows, 1995
Winter Barnyard, 1995 (overleaf)

179

Robert Bateman

human element were removed or transformed. In the rush toward economic globalization and the social homogenization it encourages, we are losing something precious and possibly irretrievable.

Back in 1967, when I prepared my first art show to mark the celebration of Canada's centennial year, I chose as subjects a series of human-made artifacts that had survived the previous hundred years. In Halton County just west of Toronto, where I then lived, such subjects were not difficult to find: old barns, Victorian farmhouses, wooden pumps and split-rail fences were there in abundance. Now, with the exception of an old chapel, everything I painted is gone.

I certainly don't claim to have any magic solutions to the problems we confront as a species and as a planet. But I am enough of an optimist to believe that solutions do exist. The real problems facing our planet are not economic or technical, they are philosophical. I firmly believe that the basis for any solution will be a change in values away from our worship of consumption and convenience. It may sound trite, but I think this saying is profoundly true: where there's a will there's a way, but if there's no will, there's no way.

What kind of world will your grandchildren and mine inherit? I pray it will be at least half as rich and varied as the one that was bequeathed to me.

Early Spring – Bluebird, 1982
Day Lilies and Dragonflies, 1991 (overleaf)

Epilogue

For thousands of years before the arrival of Europeans, the inhabitants of the northwest Pacific coast lived in harmony with their environment. If they needed a big tree for a house or a totem or a canoe, they chose it with care and harvested it with great respect. Before cutting down the tree, they held a ceremony and said prayers of appreciation and thanksgiving and apology. I've sometimes wondered what effect it would have on our forestry practices if each time a huge forest-products company cut down an ancient old-growth Sitka spruce or Douglas fir or red cedar, it had to convene a special meeting of the board of directors to honor the tree's long life and ask its forgiveness.

The fate of the human race ultimately depends on the health of our planet, and that health depends on the preservation of biological diversity. Contrary to science fiction fantasy, there won't be a convenient new world to move to after we've destroyed this one. But perhaps the most profound reason for changing our values and our behavior has to do with simple morality. The other living things with whom we share the biosphere have as much right to be here as we do. We demonstrate colossal arrogance by assuming that all other species were placed on earth as resources for us to exploit, that their lives are necessarily less valuable than our own.

I believe the solutions to our current problems are all around us: in the untapped genetic storehouse of the rainforest, in the wisdom of indigenous peoples and in the rising environmental consciousness of young people. These solutions won't be easy to implement, and they won't come cheap, but I'm sure the effort and expense will be worthwhile. I can't imagine anything more complex, varied and beautiful than the planet earth—or anything more worth saving.

Self-portrait with Big Machine and Ancient Sitka, 1993

Index to the Paintings and Drawings

108,109 *Picnic Table – Pileated Woodpeckers*, 1987★
12” x 18”; acrylic

110 *Morning Cove – Common Loon*, 1988★
10” x 16 1/2”; acrylic

111 *Rocky Point, October*, 1987★
11 7/8” x 17 7/8”; acrylic

112 *Fall – Ovenbird*, 1991
8” x 12”; acrylic

113 *Cape May Warbler and Balsam*, 1992★
13 7/8” x 10 1/2”; acrylic

114,115 *Mangrove Shadow – Common Egret*, 1991★
25 7/8” x 36”; acrylic

116 *Venice Train Station*, 1991
18” x 24”; acrylic

117 *Great Egret Preening*, 1986★
40” x 27”; acrylic

118 *Gulf Coast – Laughing Gulls*, 1991★
18” x 24”; acrylic

119 *Egret and Full Moon*, 1991
18” x 9 1/2”; acrylic

120,121 *King Vulture*, 1995
12” x 16”; oil

122 *Mayan and Hut*, 1994
10 1/4” x 14 1/2”; mixed media

123 *Chiclero*, 1994
12” x 9 1/2”; acrylic

125 *Under the Canopy – Keel-billed Toucan*, 1994★
30” x 24”; acrylic

126,127 *Symbol of the Rainforest – Spotted Jaguar*, 1994★
16” x 30”; oil/acrylic

128,129 *Reclining Ocelot*, 1994★
14” x 28”; acrylic

129 *Sitting Ocelot*, 1995
12” x 16”; oil

130 *Quetzal*, 1993★
19” x 12 3/4”; acrylic

131 *Rainforest – Swallow-tailed Kite*, 1994
24” x 18”; acrylic

132,133 *Shadow of the Rainforest – Black Jaguar*, 1992★
24” x 36”; acrylic

134,135 *Path of the Panther*, 1993★
24” x 36”; oil

136,137 *Indian Rhinoceros*, 1995
24” x 48”; gouache

138 *Sumatran Tiger*, 1995
12 1/2” x 17 3/4”; acrylic

139 *Land Rover Campsite in Bamboo*, 1958
4” x 9”; watercolor

140 *Ba Mbuti Pygmies*, 1958
5” x 5 1/2”; watercolor

141 *Malaysian Aboriginal*, 1996
13 1/8” x 8 3/4”; acrylic

141 *Senoi Huts*, 1958
13 3/4” x 9 3/4”; watercolor

142 *Macaque Family*, 1995
12 1/4” x 15 1/2”; acrylic

142,143 *Tokyo Pond – Spotbilled Ducks*, 1995★
15 1/2” x 30”; acrylic

144,145 *Cries of Courtship – Red-crowned Cranes*, 1991★
58 1/4” x 93 7/8”; acrylic

146,147 *Old Willow – Mandarin Pair*, 1995★
17” x 36”; acrylic

148 *Pandas at Play*, 1988★
5 7/8” x 18”; lithograph

149 *Giant Panda in the Wild*, 1993★
16” x 12”; acrylic

150,151 *Winter Filigree – Giant Panda*, 1995★
24” x 36”; acrylic

152 *Snowy Nap – Tiger*, 1993★
15” x 20”; mixed media

152,153 *Siberian Tiger*, 1991★
31 3/4” x 47 7/8”; acrylic

154,155 *Sudden Move – Siberian Tiger*, 1995★
30” x 60”; acrylic

156,157 *Tembo*, 1990★
72” x 96”; oil

157 *Baby Elephant Drawing*, 1988
10” x 12”; graphite

158 *African Amber – Lioness Pair*, 1977★
24” x 42”; acrylic

159 *Passing Fancy – Lion Cubs and Rhino*, 1992
18” x 24”; acrylic

160,161 *Dispute Over Prey*, 1975★
32” x 48”; acrylic

162 *Pensive Moment – Juvenile Gorilla*, 1995
16” x 11 3/4”; gouache

162,163 *Intrusion – Mountain Gorilla*, 1992★
26 7/8” x 37 3/8”; acrylic

164 *Israeli Leopard*, 1995
12 1/2” x 17 3/4”; acrylic

165 *Ibex at Masada Study*, 1996
8 7/8” x 11 7/8”; acrylic

166 *Stork and Well, Sieburczyn*, 1992
12” x 8”; acrylic

167 *Polish Stableyard*, 1993
24” x 36”; acrylic

168 *Spanish Pig*, 1995★
24” x 48”; gouache

169 *Stone Curlew and Rock*, 1994
12” x 18”; alkyd

170,171 *Fox at the Granary*, 1975★
24 1/8” x 35 7/8”; acrylic

172 *Country Lane – Pheasant*, 1979★
16” x 20”; oil

173 *Backlight – Mute Swan*, 1989★
16” x 24 3/16”; acrylic

174 *Red Grouse in Grass*, 1994
9” x 13 7/8”; oil

175 *Little Owl on Stone Fence*, 1994
12” x 18”; alkyd

176,177 *Grandfather's Farm and Groundhog*, 1995
12” x 22 3/4”; gouache

178 *At the Bridge – Cliff Swallows*, 1995★
18” x 27”; acrylic

180,181 *Winter Barnyard*, 1995★
18” x 40”; acrylic

182,183 *Early Spring – Bluebird*, 1982★
20” x 36”; acrylic

184,185 *Day Lilies and Dragonflies*, 1991★
10” x 24”; acrylic

186 *Self-portrait with Big Machine and Ancient Sitka*, 1993
72” x 72”; acrylic
Photo by Birgit Freybe Bateman

192 *Tadpole Time*, 1984★
12” x 18”; acrylic

★These works, as well as other paintings by Robert Bateman, are available as limited-edition prints by Mill Pond Press. For more information about their print publishing program please direct inquiries to the appropriate address:

In the United States

Mill Pond Press
310 Center Court
Venice, Florida   34292-3500

In Canada

Nature's Scene
976 Meyerside Drive, Unit #1
Mississauga, Ontario
L5T 1R9

In the United Kingdom

Solomon & Whitehead Ltd.
Lynn Lane, Shenstone
Nr. Lichfield, Staffs.
England   WS14 0DX

Robert Bateman: A Chronology

1930 — Born May 24 in Toronto, Ontario, Canada, to Joseph Wilberforce Bateman and Annie Maria Bateman (née McLellan). He is the first of three children; brothers John (Jack) and Ross are born in 1933 and 1936.

1935-45 — Attends primary and elementary school.

1938 — Bateman family rents and eventually purchases a summer cottage in the Haliburton lakes region of Ontario. Time spent here is an important part of Bob's development as an artist and naturalist.

1942 — Joins the Junior Field Naturalist's Club at the Royal Ontario Museum. During his teen years there he develops his birdwatching skills and ornithological knowledge under the influence of James L. Baillie and Terence Shortt. Shortt, an outstanding bird painter, is a major and long-lasting influence.

1945-50 — Attends high school at Forest Hill Collegiate in Toronto. During high school he is active in the Biology Club of the University of Toronto.

1947-49 — Spends three summers working at a government wildlife research camp in Algonquin Park in northern Ontario. Here his enthusiasm for the landscapes of the painters of the Canadian Group of Seven grows.

1948 — Begins taking painting lessons from Gordon Payne, a well-respected Toronto artist, who teaches him the basic skills of representational painting.

1950 — After graduating from high school travels to Vancouver Island by bus, painting and sketching with his friend Erik Thorn.

1950-54 — Attends the University of Toronto in a four-year honors course in geography. Also takes evening courses in the Nikolaides method of drawing from Carl Schaefer. Summer jobs on geological field parties take him to Newfoundland, Ungava Bay and Hudson Bay.

1954 — Graduates from university and takes a painting and sketching tour of Europe and Scandinavia.

1954-63 — Experiments with a range of painting styles. From the influence of Impressionism and the Canadian Group of Seven, he moves into a cubist phase, and, finally, embraces an abstract-expressionist style.

1955 — Receives a teaching certificate from the Ontario College of Education and begins a career as a high-school teacher of geography and art in Thornhill, Ontario.

1957-58 — A round-the-world trip in a Land Rover with friend Bristol Foster takes him to England, Africa, India, Sikkim, Burma, Thailand, Malaysia and Australia.

1958 — Resumes his teaching career in Burlington, Ontario.

1960 — Marries Suzanne Bowerman, a sculpture student at the Ontario College of Art.

1962 — Attends a major Andrew Wyeth exhibition at the Albright-Knox Gallery in Buffalo, New York. This encourages him to return to a realistic style of painting.

1963-65 — Spends two years teaching in Nigeria under the sponsorship of Canada's External Aid program. Here he begins painting African wildlife in a natural style and begins exhibiting at the Fonville Gallery in Nairobi.

1965 — A first child, Alan, is born in Nigeria. Later in the year the family returns to Canada, where Bateman resumes teaching in Burlington, Ontario. He continues to paint African wildlife for the Fonville Gallery in Kenya and begins painting Ontario landscapes and rural settings in a realistic style.

1966 — A second child, Sarah, is born.

1967 — A series of historical scenes of Halton County, Ontario, are painted as the artist's own Canadian Centennial project and are shown at the Alice Peck Gallery in Burlington, Ontario.

1968 — John, the third Bateman child, is born.

1969 — A one-man show held at the Pollock Gallery in Toronto is the first in a series of successful one-man shows.

1971 — A well-received show is staged at the Beckett Gallery in Hamilton, Ontario.

1972 — The film *Robert Bateman* is produced by the Canadian Broadcasting Corporation (CBC) for the TV series *This Land*.

1975 — A large Bateman show at the Tryon Gallery in London, England, one of the world's foremost galleries of wildlife art, is sold out. This convinces Bateman that he should paint full time.

— *Animals in Art*, a group exhibition at the Royal Ontario Museum in the same year, brings his work to Canadian attention.

— Marries Birgit Freybe, artist and high-school art teacher, after his first marriage ends in divorce.

1976 — A fourth child, Christopher, is born.

1977 — Awarded Queen Elizabeth's Silver Jubilee Medal (Canada).

1978 — Shows are held at the Beckett Gallery in Hamilton, Ontario, and the Art Gallery of Hamilton.

— Mill Pond Press begins distributing Bateman images as limited-edition, signed prints. Over 500 Bateman paintings have become prints since this program was launched.

— *Images of the Wild: A Portrait of Robert Bateman* is produced by the National Film Board of Canada.

— Travels to the Falkland Islands and the Antarctic aboard the Lindblad *Explorer*.

1979 — A fifth child, Robert, is born.

— Bateman receives the Award of Merit from the Society of Animal Artists.

1980 — Drawing lots for paintings is required at sold-out shows at the Beckett Gallery and at the Sportsman's Edge Gallery in New York City.

— Bateman is named Artist of the Year by *American Artist* magazine.

1981 — *Images of the Wild*, a major Bateman show organized by the National Museum of Natural Sciences, opens at the National Museum of Canada, Ottawa, Ontario, and travels to the Musée de Québec, Quebec City, Quebec; the Manitoba Museum of Natural History, Winnipeg, Manitoba; the Vancouver Museum, Vancouver, British Columbia; and the Royal Ontario Museum, Toronto, Ontario, over the next two years.

— *Northern Reflections – Loon Family*, a painting commissioned by the Governor General of Canada, is the official wedding gift of the people of Canada to Prince Charles.

— *The Art of Robert Bateman*, a large-format art book featuring over eighty color reproductions of Bateman paintings, with an introduction by Roger Tory Peterson and a text by Ramsay Derry, is published.

— The film *The Nature Art of Robert Bateman* is produced by Eco-Art Productions.

1982 — Bateman and three of his children visit the game parks of East Africa.

— Awarded Doctor of Science, *honoris causa*, Carleton University, Ottawa, Ontario.

— Awarded Doctor of Laws (for Fine Arts), *honoris causa*, Brock University, St. Catharines, Ontario.

1983 — The *Images of the Wild* exhibit opens at the California Academy of Sciences in San Francisco, and eventually travels to the

St. Louis Museum of Natural History, St. Louis; the Cleveland Museum of Natural History, Cleveland; the Cincinnati Museum of Natural History, Cincinnati; the Greenville Art Museum, Greenville, South Carolina; the Frye Art Museum, Seattle, Washington; and ends its tour in 1991 at the Colorado Springs Fine Arts Center, Colorado Springs, Colorado.

— Awarded Doctor of Letters (for Fine Arts), *honoris causa*, McMaster University, Hamilton, Ontario.

— *Robert Bateman: A Celebration of Nature* produced for the CBC television series *Take 30*.

1984 — Bateman is named an officer of the Order of Canada.

— *Robert Bateman: Artist and Naturalist*, a one-hour television documentary, is shown on the CBC.

— Awarded Doctor of Laws, *honoris causa*, University of Guelph, Guelph, Ontario.

1985 — The Tryon Gallery in London exhibits a major Bateman show.

— *The World of Robert Bateman*, a second book devoted to the work of Robert Bateman, is published.

— Bateman is awarded the Medal of Honor, World Wildlife Fund, Geneva (presented by HRH Prince Philip).

— The Batemans move to Fulford Harbour, Salt Spring Island, British Columbia.

1986 — One-man shows are held at the Gilcrease Art Museum, Tulsa, Oklahoma; the Leigh Yawkey Woodson Art Museum, Wausau, Wisconsin; the Beckett Gallery, Hamilton, Ontario; and the Joslyn Art Museum, Omaha, Nebraska.

— Bateman is awarded Doctor of Letters (for Fine Arts), *honoris causa*, Lakehead University, Thunder Bay, Ontario.

1987 — The *Portraits of Nature* exhibit opens at the Smithsonian Institution's Museum of Natural History in Washington, D.C.

— Awarded Doctor of Laws, Laurentian University, Sudbury, Ontario.

— Bateman is awarded the Governor General's Award for Conservation, Quebec City, Quebec.

— Spends the year in Bavaria.

1988 — The *Images of the Wild — The Art of Robert Bateman* exhibit opens at the Frye Art Museum, Seattle, Washington.

— Visits Japan, China, Nepal and India.

1989 — Paints *Charging Grizzly* as a birthday present for Prince Bernhard of the Netherlands.

— Bateman is awarded Doctor of Fine Arts, *honoris causa*, Colby College, Waterville, Maine.

1990 — *Robert Bateman: An Artist in Nature*, a third book featuring Bateman as artist, naturalist and conservationist, is published.

1991 — The Beckett Gallery in Hamilton, Ontario, exhibits a major Bateman show.

— Awarded Doctor of Fine Arts, *honoris causa*, Northeastern University, Boston, Massachusetts.

— The *Natural World* show opens at the Canadian embassy in Japan and eventually travels as *Natural Visions* to the Carnegie Museum of Natural History, Pittsburgh, Pennsylvania; the California Academy of Sciences, San Francisco, California; the Los Angeles Museum of Natural History, Los Angeles, California; the Vancouver Museum, Vancouver, British Columbia; and the Art Gallery of Greater Victoria, Victoria, British Columbia.

— Robert Bateman Elementary School opens in Ottawa, Ontario.

1992 — Travels to Poland for the Artists for Nature Foundation.

1993 — Visits Belize, Germany, Holland, Alaska, Tanzania, Kenya, Zaire and Indonesia.

1994 — Travels to Spain for the Artists for Nature Foundation.

— The Arizona Sonora Desert Museum exhibits a show of Bateman original prints and paintings.

— The one-hour video *Robert Bateman* released by the Art Gallery of Greater Victoria.

— Robert Bateman Secondary School opens in Abbotsford, British Columbia.

— Visits Belize, Antarctica, Papua New Guinea, Greenland and Baffin Island.

1995 — The *Canadian Wildlife Artists* exhibit, featuring the paintings of Robert Bateman and four other Canadian artists, opens at the Suntory Museum, Osaka, Japan.

— Bateman is awarded Doctor of Science, *honoris causa*, McGill University, Montreal, Quebec.

1996 — *Natural Worlds*, the fourth book devoted to the work of Robert Bateman, is published.

— Visits Africa, India and Alaska.

Acknowledgments

My collaborations with Robert Bateman over the past decade have invariably been pleasurable and mind-expanding. Writing the text for *Natural Worlds* has been no exception. Bob and his wife, Birgit, have welcomed me in their home and been generous with their time, knowledge and expertise. The indefatigable and unfailingly cheerful Jane Reid and Alex Fischer, who administer the Bateman office and organize Bob's life, responded with alacrity to my endless requests for more information.

As usual, many others contributed their time and expertise. Above all, I'd like to acknowledge Ron Ridout, of the Long Point Bird Observatory, and Bristol Foster, wildlife biologist and naturalist extraordinaire, for acting as consultants on the project and vetting the entire text. I'd also like to extend special thanks to Jeff Kenney of World Wildlife Fund Canada for his instant responses to my often picayune questions and for putting me in touch with many of the experts I needed to consult. These experts, many of whom commented on the text, have contributed enormously to its breadth and accuracy. (Any errors that remain are mine.) I would like to thank them as follows:

Nathalie Macfarlane of the Queen Charlotte Islands Museum; Amanda Brown of the Gwaalagaa Naay Corporation; Peter Macnair of the Royal British Columbia Museum; Jim Borrowman of Chubb Island Charters; Alexandra Morton of Raincoast Research; Skip McKinnell of Fisheries and Oceans Canada; Catherine Stewart of Greenpeace; Steven Brechtel of Alberta Environmental Protection; Barry Adams of Alberta Natural Resources, Agriculture, Food and Rural Development; William Koonz of Natural Resources Manitoba; Alan Smith, Philip Taylor and Brenda Dale of the Canadian Wildlife Service; Paul James of the Saskatchewan Museum of Natural History; James Lewis of the U.S. Fish and Wildlife Service; Harry Lumsden of the Ontario Trumpeter Swan Restoration Group; Marcia Sullivan of the Mexican Wolf Coalition of Texas; Axel Moehrenschlager of Oxford University; Fred Cooke of Simon Fraser University; Jim Allan of Ecosummer Expeditions; The Rainforest Action Network; The Nature Reserves Authority of Israel; Wilf Wakely, of the Province of British Columbia Trade Development Corporation in Japan; Mark Ross of Geosafaris Limited.

A special nod to John Lee, for his equanimity in the face of countless text changes and conceptual rethinks—and for his splendid design. And particular thanks to Kathryn Dean, a true professional, for her acute, astute and judicious copy editing.

Finally, I'd like to acknowledge the staff at Madison Press, whose support has been as always superb, especially my deft and diplomatic editor Mireille Majoor; Hugh Brewster, who always kept the long-term goal in view; and Sandra Hall, who provided energetic organizational support and tracked down many elusive paintings.

—Rick Archbold

Madison Press Books would like to thank Linda Schaner of Mill Pond Press for her invaluable advice, assistance, humor and expertise; Ysbrand Brouwers of the Artists for Nature Foundation for supplying transparencies; and all of the owners of original Bateman artwork who so generously allowed images to be photographed for this book.

Tadpole Time, 1984

Design and Art Direction: V. John Lee
Editorial Director: Hugh M. Brewster
Project Editor: Mireille Majoor
Editorial Assistant: Lloyd Davis
Production Director: Susan Barrable
Production Co-ordinator: Sandra L. Hall
Printing and Binding: Imago Productions (F.E.) Ltd., Singapore

ROBERT BATEMAN: NATURAL WORLDS
was produced by Madison Press Books.